THE OBJECTIVE
PSYCHE

THE OBJECTIVE PSYCHE

by

MICHAEL FORDHAM
M.D., M.R.C.P., F.B.Ps.S.

Routledge and Kegan Paul
LONDON

First published 1958
by Routledge & Kegan Paul Ltd
*Broadway House, Carter Lane, E.C.*4
Printed in Great Britain
by Western Printing Services Ltd, Bristol

CONTENTS

v

ACKNOWLEDGMENTS

I WISH to acknowledge with gratitude the permission given by the editors to publish papers previously published in or by the British Journal of Medical Psychology, the International Journal of Social Psychiatry, the Revue suisse de Psychologie et de Psychologie appliquée, the British Medical Bulletin, the Guild of Pastoral Psychology; also to the Analytical Psychology Club for allowing me to publish the paper read to its members in 1944.

I

INTRODUCTION

IN 1944 a group of analysts started to form a professional organization. They aimed at founding a centre where information about the theory of analytical psychology and training in its practice would be made available. Such was the origin of the Society of Analytical Psychology, which soon met with a good reception.

Since that time the increase in the number of analysts has begun to result in new trends and specialized interests amongst its members. Some of my own researches have been published in two volumes: *The Life of Childhood* (London, 1944) and *New Developments in Analytical Psychology* (London, 1957). The essays in the present volume are less specialized than and complement the latter book; the three publications give a fair account of my contribution between 1944 and 1957.

In the recent edition of *The New Outline of Modern Knowledge*,[1] Jung's researches were moved from the section on science to that on religion and the arts. This change marks a trend to be found inside as well as outside the ranks of analytical psychologists. With the intention of counteracting it, I have altered the first paper, originally written in 1945, so as to give more consideration to Jung's scientific standing. On the whole the tendency to play down the scientific nature of his work has led to a tendency to depreciate thought and sometimes a loose application of theory to practice.

It may be that the belief in analytical psychology as more a religion than a science arises in those who become overawed by the numinous character of the archetypal images; they then overestimate dream psychology and active imagination. This can lead and has led to a neglect of theory in the spheres of personal, ego, and child psychology, and to overlooking the importance of the

[1] London, 1956. Editor, A. Pryce-Jones.

B   I

transference in analytical practice. My studies aim at compensating this trend.

In contrast to the low scientific estimate in which analytical psychology is held by some, there has arisen a movement of a different kind. This stems mainly from Catholic theologians, and R. Hostie, S.J.,[2] may be singled out from other more cautious writers. So as to limit the influence of archetypal psychology upon religion, he uses Jung's scientific status to construct a boundary between theology and psychology. In doing this, however, he inevitably sets an arbitrary limit to the spirit of scientific inquiry; a view which few scientists would accept, and I am not one of them. The thesis that the boundaries between religion and psychology should be kept open is elaborated in the three essays on religious topics; they also reveal my distaste for esoteric tendencies.

Up to now I have not made any serious attempt to bring my researches into specific relation with the process of individuation. In two essays written for this volume, I have begun to fill in an obvious gap: one, 'Individuation and Ego Development', is theoretical; it is followed by 'Problems of Active Imagination', in which I have applied the concept of the first to clinical procedures. Together the essays aim at showing the importance of keeping concepts in close relation to the empirical study of human beings.

In recent years considerable changes have occurred in psychoanalysis in Great Britain. These have made it desirable to relate its newer formulations to those of analytical psychology, though it would, I think, be premature to reassess the position of the two schools, particularly as each one has on the whole become less rather than more coherent. The scattered references to such psycho-analysts as W. R. Bion, Melanie Klein, Mrs. Milner, Clifford Scott and D. W. Winnicott indicate the interest which the researches of these analysts have aroused in me, mainly as the result of discussions which took place in the Medical Section of the British Psychological Society.

As a whole I recognize that the present volume may be criticized for the preponderance of theoretical arguments and for the frequent lack of supporting evidence for its contentions. I intend to emphasize the need for more careful analysis of concepts

[2] *Religion and the Psychology of Jung*. London and New York, 1957.

derived from already published material; the need for disciplined analytical thought is evident at the present time. However, the day-to-day contact with patients in analytical practice, where the irrationality of human beings is so much in evidence, does not lead me to believe that organized thought alone will ever prove adequate in any psychological discipline which aims at expressing the wholeness of man.

II

THE DEVELOPMENT AND STATUS
OF JUNG'S RESEARCHES[1]

INTRODUCTION

CARL GUSTAV JUNG was born on 26 July 1875, the son
of a Swiss pastor and philologist of Basel, Switzerland; he
is one of a select number of pioneers who have, in the last
half-century, laid the foundations of a scientific psychology of the
unconscious. His path has taken him into regions where science
had not previously been applied with success,[2] and again and
again many have supposed him lost to its disciplines. I believe
that their view is mistaken. His grasp of scientific method has
always formed the basis of his researches and they have an inner
consistency which it is the object of this paper to reveal.

Jung is first and foremost an investigator, and therefore many
of his theories have been altered or abandoned as they proved
inadequate to the phenomena under consideration. This appears
to bewilder some of his readers, who mistakenly expect a logically
coherent structure, but in a germinating science this could not be
attained. In any case Jung is no system builder, as he realizes
when he says

it is my firm conviction that the time for an all-inclusive theory, taking
in and presenting all the contents, processes and phenomena of the
psyche from one central viewpoint, has not yet come by a long way. I
regard my theories as suggestions and attempts at the formulation of a
new scientific concept of psychology based, in the first place, upon
immediate experience with human beings.[3]

[1] Originally 'C. G. Jung', *British Journal of Medical Psychology*, Vol.
XX, No. 3 (1945), pp. 221 ff. First published in honour of Professor
Jung's seventieth birthday, this paper has been altered and adapted to the
needs of the present volume, though its framework has been retained.

[2] Particularly occultism.

[3] Foreword to J. Jacobi, *The Psychology of C. G. Jung*. Trans. by K. W.
Bash. London, 1942.

4

Jung's first idea was to become an archaeologist, but this was stillborn; its occurrence is interesting, however, because of its symbolic reference. Evidently this is the first intimation, in a different form, of his later psychological 'excavations' into the collective unconscious.

His first realized professional aim was to study medicine and he qualified as a doctor in 1900. Psychiatry had not attracted him; on the contrary, it was assumed that he would take up physiological chemistry for which he had shown a special aptitude. One day, however, he picked up Krafft-Ebing's *Text-Book of Psychiatry*, reading it, with scarcely any break, from cover to cover. This book exercised a determining influence on his career, and led him to take a post as second assistant at the Burghölzli Asylum at Zurich, where he was at first the student and then the collaborator of Eugen Bleuler. This association lasted until 1909, two years after his meeting with Freud.

1902–1907

Jung's first published work was *On the Psychology and Pathology of So-called Occult Phenomena*,[4] which appeared in 1902;[5] it is the study of an adolescent girl, S.W., fifteen and a half years of age. There was a history of instability in her family but her development appears to have been relatively normal until she discovered her 'mediumistic' powers at a table-turning session. She developed hysterical trances during which various 'spirits' appeared. Amongst them were 'Ulrich Gerbenstein', a witty, idle gambler, whose outstanding characteristic was his superficiality, and 'Ivenes', a serious, mature, sexually prolific and dignified woman, who was specially related to the 'other side' or spirit world from which she received messages. The mediumistic sessions, which went on for about a year, culminated in the revelation of a system of 'world forces' of which S.W. made a diagram of special interest in view of Jung's later researches: 'In the centre stands the Primary Force; this is the original cause of creation and is a spiritual force.'[6] Around it were seven circles

[4] Cf. *Psychiatric Studies* (Collected Works of C. G. Jung, Vol. I). London and New York, 1957.

[5] Dates of Jung's works given in the text invariably refer to publication of the first edition in German.

[6] Op. cit., pp. 40–41.

depicting natural forces. There were three other circles whose contents were not sufficiently definite to be clearly represented. The figure was divided into four equal parts by two diagonal lines; it is what we now know as a mandala. Following her revelation, the trances gradually diminished in frequency and 'Ulrich Gerbenstein' came more and more to the fore. Eventually S.W. was found to be cheating and so appeared valueless for scientific purposes, but her later development was particularly satisfactory inasmuch as she became a capable and industrious business woman. In short, the process begun by the table turning reached a climax which occurred at the same time as the appearance of the 'revelation'.

In his theoretical discussion, which clearly shows the influence of Pierre Janet,[7] whom he visited in 1902 and 1903, Jung starts from the idea that 'Ivenes' is the 'extension' of S.W.'s personality whose emergence into consciousness made possible the satisfactory adaptation in later life. He says: 'It is, therefore, conceivable that the phenomena of double consciousness are simply new character formations, or attempts of the future personality to break through. . . .'[8] Thus in 1902 two concepts were formulated which became the basis for his later studies: first, the essential importance of consciousness, and second, the synthetic or prospective nature of the unconscious contents. It is apparent that neurotic phenomena were regarded by Jung in his first publication as positive, emergent events, an idea which he subsequently developed and expressed as follows:

The symptoms of a neurosis are not simply the effects of long-past causes, whether 'infantile sexuality' or the infantile urge to power; they are also attempts at a new synthesis of life—unsuccessful attempts, let it be added in the same breath, yet attempts nevertheless, with a core of value and meaning. They are seeds that fail to sprout owing to the inclement conditions of an inner and outer nature.[9]

[7] This can be recognized in the concept of suggestion and the use of hypnotism, which were soon abandoned in favour of psycho-analysis, whilst such phrases adopted from Janet as 'abaissement du niveau mental' and 'les parties supérieure et inférieure' are used by Jung even in his latest publications.

[8] Op. cit., p. 79.

[9] 'The Problem of the Attitude-Type.' *Two Essays on Analytical Psychology* (Collected Works, Vol. VII). London and New York, 1953, p. 45.

These interesting conclusions are not, however, the most important consequences of the first research which gave Jung an aim that he never relinquished. He saw that the case material could not be understood in terms of current psychiatric theories; his reading had already led him to philosophy, to Schopenhauer and von Hartmann, and it was from these sources that he derived the concept of the unconscious which provided him with what he needed. He set himself the aim of converting the idea from a philosophical to a scientific concept.

A thoroughgoing empiricist, Jung could never rest content with an abstract discipline; he needed facts upon which to ground and test his hypotheses. Thus it was the study of his first case which awoke his interest in the occult as a whole, but also, and far more important, it led him on to use the experimental method in order to test the hypothesis of unconscious complexes which he had formulated as an explanation of the mediumistic phenomena.

The instrument he needed, the association tests, had already been constructed by Galton in England and refined in the Kraepelinian school by Aschaffenberg, who had devised a classification of associations of which Jung made use. The classification had been rendered necessary by the great variation in response to stimulus words, but no conclusions had been drawn from the study of those peculiarities which could not be classified. It took Jung to grasp their significance and to discover that they were the consequence, not of meaningless activity but of an affect hidden from the investigator though capable of being deduced by him and confirmed by the subject. The confirmation, however, was not always easy. Sometimes it could be arrived at by questioning, sometimes by confronting the patient with the conclusion; where it could not be confirmed in this way, Jung found the solution by using Freud's method of free association.[10] Thus he was not only the first to gain access to the unconscious experimentally, but also the first to attempt validation of the findings of psycho-analysis by using test procedures. In a later paper[11] he discusses illuminatingly the limits of experiment in the investigation of unconscious processes.

[10] 'Psycho-analysis and Association Experiments'. *Studies in Word Association*. London, 1918; New York, 1919.

[11] 'Allgemeines zur Komplextheorie'. *Über psychische Energetik und das Wesen der Träume*. Zurich, 1948.

The completion of these investigations represents the fufilment of Jung's first aim; he had succeeded in demonstrating the existence of unconscious complexes. The association studies also contained the germs of his type theory, which is hinted at in the analysis of Aschaffenberg's classification.

Besides the use of association experiments to establish the theory of complexes, mention may here be made of Jung's early studies in psychopathology which gave rise to papers on such subjects as simulated insanity in criminals, hysteria, chronic mania, epilepsy, and, far the most important, the study of dementia praecox,[12] in which he used the association tests to penetrate into the meaning of the psychotic phenomena; this now standard work became, together with Freud's later researches, the foundation for all psycho-dynamic understanding of schizophrenia.[13]

1907–1914

It was inevitable that Jung's researches should lead him to a closer association with Freud, and he began the second fateful period in his development by becoming an enthusiastic advocate of psycho-analysis. Psycho-analysis could provide him with just the wealth of factual material for which he was looking, and in its advocacy he risked his good name and ruined his professional prospects. In 1907 he went to Vienna; he was at once deeply impressed by Freud, and an intimate relationship, founded on

[12] The background of Jung's early psychiatric studies has been interestingly discussed by Professor Aubrey Lewis in relation to current trends in psychiatry. Cf. 'Jung's Early Work', *Journal of Analytical Psychology*, Vol. II, No. 2, 1957, pp. 119 ff. The papers he there refers to are mostly to be found in *Psychiatric Studies* (Collected Works, Vol. I). London and New York, 1957.

[13] *The Psychology of Dementia Praecox*. London, 1909. This early work on the psychoses undoubtedly influenced the course of Jung's development and assisted him towards his subsequent discoveries. In *The Integration of the Personality*, London, 1940, when discussing the theories of Freud and Adler, he writes (p. 6): 'Both theories are based chiefly upon experience with cases of neurosis. Neither of the authors had any psychiatric experience. If they had, they would certainly have been impressed with the fact that the unconscious displays certain contents that are utterly different from those of consciousness; such strange ones, indeed, that nobody can understand them, neither the patient himself nor his doctors.'

mutual respect, began.[14] In 1909 he went with him to the United States and lectured at Clark University on his association experiments conducted on normal and pathological individuals; in the same year, together with Freud and Bleuler, he founded the *Jahrbuch für Psychoanalytische und Psychopathologische Forschungen*, and in 1910 he became the first president of the International Psycho-Analytical Association. During this time his proposal that analysts should themselves be analysed, before undertaking the treatment of patients, was seconded by Freud and adopted by the Psycho-Analytical Association; it has been adhered to ever since, and has become the basis of all analytical training.

Jung's published contributions to psycho-analysis, apart from his critical estimation of it, and of course *The Psychology of the Unconscious* to be considered separately, show germs of new developments running alongside experimental studies. His more significant publications were as follows: 'The Association Method',[15] being the lectures delivered at Clark University in 1909, mainly noteworthy for a study of sexual development in a little girl, Anna; 'The Significance of the Father in the Destiny of the Individual' (1909),[16] introducing the idea of fate and inevitability which later became more clearly defined as a transpersonal phenomenon; 'On the Significance of Number Dreams' (1911),[17] which is of particular interest because number symbolism later became a central feature of self images and has been revived again in a new form in the recently published essay on synchronicity;[18] there was also 'The Psychology of Rumour' (1910),[19] 'The Content of the Psychoses' (1914),[20] and a number of other shorter essays and critical works. The correspondence with Dr. Loy entitled 'Some Crucial Points in Psychoanalysis' (1913)[21] needs special mention. It is of interest because it discusses the relation between hypnotism, suggestion therapy, and the transference.

[14] Cf. E. Jones, *Sigmund Freud, Life and Work*, Vol. II. London, 1955.
[15] In *Collected Papers on Analytical Psychology*, edited by Constance Long. 2nd edition. London, 1917; New York, 1920.
[16] Ibid.   [17] Ibid.
[18] Jung, 'Synchronicity: An Acausal Connecting Principle', in C. G. Jung and W. Pauli, *The Interpretation af Nature and the Psyche*. London and New York, 1955.
[19] In *Collected Papers* (see note 15).   [20] Ibid.   [21] Ibid.

In 1914, four years after the International Association was founded, Jung gave up the title of psycho-analyst to form his own school of analytical psychology. The break with Freud marks the end of the second period. Viewed in retrospect it seems inevitable that Freud and Jung should separate, especially if we consider the occultist background of it all to which, Jones[22] claims, Jung and Ferenczi were heartily committed and in which Freud participated; I cannot believe it was not the conditions in those early days of psycho-analysis[23] that determined the break, perhaps more than ever the clash of personalities holding incompatible scientific theories.[24]

The effect of psycho-analysis upon Jung may be summed up by saying that it changed him from a psychiatrist into an analyst. It gave him tools with which to make the discoveries especially associated with his name. Considering this period in his development carefully, it can be seen that his writings before, during, and while he was a leading psycho-analyst, contain essential disagreements with Freud, of which the theory of psychic energy was perhaps the most important. It should be remembered that its first formulation was completed not after, but before his meeting with Freud in 1907; from the beginning he doubted the value of extending the sexual theory so far as Freud insisted on doing.

It is sometimes said that Jung's researches of the early period are unimportant. I can only say that, to me, they are essential, at least if his method of approach and attitude to analytic practice is to be understood; and it is there, after all, that the foundations of analytical psychology lie. It may be claimed that neither psycho-analysis nor analytical psychology are what they were then, but the present state of affairs carries with it a historical development throwing the essential features of each discipline into relief. If the basic trends in Jung's works are to be understood, a longitudinal study of his writings is of the greatest

[22] Cf. Jones, 'Occultism', *Sigmund Freud, Life and Work*, Vol. III. London, 1957.

[23] Cf. E. Neumann, 'In Honour of the Centenary of Freud's Birth', *Journal of Analytical Psychology*, Vol. I, No. 2, 1956.

[24] I have refrained from commenting upon the affective content of Jung's break with Freud, since all I could say would be the rankest speculation of which there has already been enough. Jones has given an authoritative account of it from the psycho-analytic side, it is to be hoped that one day a comparable assessment will be made from Jung's standpoint.

help; but it may be added that his earlier views, which he refers to later from time to time, contain valuable clues for his followers, particularly those studying psychopathology or seeking to develop analytical techniques, which Jung left on the way as suggestions. If, therefore, more time is spent on the early periods than to some would seem warrantable, I consider that this needs no apology.

In 1913 Jung set out his view of the origin and nature of neurosis in *The Theory of Psycho-Analysis*.[25] This volume, consisting of lectures delivered in New York in September 1912, contains the first presentation of the analytical theories and practices which he had developed; since then they have changed, but much is still relevant and stimulating even though the book also contains a number of ambiguities, probably arising from an attempt to conform to psycho-analytic thinking which really violated the trends of thought developing in him.

Jung's researches with the association experiments had impressed him with the importance of what he termed the 'actual situation'. This term covers the present life situation of the patient; it contains the determining causal factor of neuroses and defines the part he believes infantile memories to play in them. A failure to adapt in the 'actual situation' can result in a regression in which memories and fantasies, not part of that situation, are regressively reactivated, and so are not a cause of the disorder. Under these circumstances they are an arrangement, a means of avoiding the actual situation of which they are not a necessary part—in this he follows Alfred Adler. On the other hand, if the infantile material is part of the actual situation it is one of the causes of the neurosis originating in infancy, to which it must be reduced, otherwise it is lived unconsciously in the present as the unadapted part of the actual situation.

But the actual situation contains more than past and present conflicts; some of it is prospective, and so Jung also focused attention on the potentialities lying hidden within the neurotic patterns; he was beginning to feel more certain of the existence

[25] New York, 1915 (Swiss version, 1913). This essay was attacked with evident animosity by Karl Abraham in 'Review of C. G. Jung's "Versuch einer Darstellung der Psychoanalytischen Theorie"' (Attempt at a Representation of the Psycho-analytic Theory), *Clinical Papers and Essays on Psycho-analysis*, London, 1955.

of 'new character formulations' and a 'future personality' within the actual situation. It was his concentration on these which gave him less and less interest in what he terms reductive analysis.

A significant part of Jung's criticism of Freud was terminological. He wanted, for instance, to change the phrase 'polymorphous perverse' to 'polymorphous predisposition' on the grounds of the generality and symbolic content of infantile sexuality of which the Oedipus pattern is a part. In doing this he radically changed Freud's meaning, bringing it more into line with general biological theory and making it conform with his theory of psychic energy. It may also be remarked that he removed the apparent negative evaluation of infantile sexuality and reserved the term perverse for the form it took when regressively reactivated. This terminological change reflects the earlier attitude of maintaining a distinction between what was normal or healthy and what abnormal or pathological. It is not a rejection of infantile sexuality as such, but a theoretical revaluation of its dual significance.

For some time Jung had been embarking upon extensive comparative studies in mythology and folklore, of which he said:[26]

From the present position of this work, we can scarcely conceive what a vast perspective may result from this comparative ethnopsychology. Through the study of mythology, we may expect the psycho-analytic knowledge of the nature of the unconscious process to be enormously enriched and deepened.

He had already written the Swiss version of *Psychology of the Unconscious* (in 1912) of which he said: 'The whole thing came upon me like a landslide that cannot be stopped. The urgency that lay behind it became clear to me only later. . . .'[27] He had taken a case of incipient schizophrenia and, analysing the material, using his newly developed comparative method, he concluded that the origin of the disorder was to be traced to a presexual fixation in the mother-child relationship and in the failure of what he called 'the Battle for Deliverance'.

This leads to a further point of difference from Freud. In the discussion of cases involving a mother fixation, Jung held that the

---

[26] *The Theory of Psychoanalysis*, p. 112.
[27] 'Foreword to the Fourth Swiss Edition', *Symbols of Transformation* (Collected Works, Vol. V). London and New York, 1956, p. i.

imagery could not possibly be accounted for on the basis of the interaction between the patient himself, as a real child, and the real mother, as Freud had maintained.[28] He therefore postulated an inherited mother imago within the psyche of the patient, having its roots in a function which he subsequently called the mother archetype. This opened the door to myth as an irreducible fact in the psyche, and Freud could not allow this because of the mystical elements to which the idea opened a door. Out of this conflict came Jung's concepts of the personal or repressed unconscious, to which, somewhat unjustly even then, he relegated Freud's investigations, and the collective unconscious, which he thought of as the layer beneath the level of Freud's discoveries.[29] With the formulation of the latter concept he had embarked upon widening the basis of psycho-analysis beyond the limits its founder considered valid, at the same time reasserting and expanding his earlier theory of psychic energy and adding to it the concept of libido symbols.

The *Psychology of the Unconscious*[30] contains the results of those researches which led to the rift with Freud. It is deeply imbued with psycho-analytic theory, but it also challenges and distorts it. Jung there penetrates into the mother archetype, where he found the libido divided into two;[31] the one part harking backward regressively in search of the mother, the other striving forward to the future.

There is no doubt that Jung considered his views a justifiable extension of Freud's work and his criticisms as legitimate

[28] This argument is concisely summarized in 'The Concept of the Collective Unconscious', *Archetypes and the Collective Unconscious* (Collected Works, Vol. IX, Part 1). London and New York, 1959. It must be remarked that here his criticism of Freud does not appear quite fair. Freud agreed much more with Jung's view than is made apparent.

[29] Thus before the synthetic processes begin it is necessary to analyse the personal unconscious to a considerable degree, and once synthetic images start to appear analysis is not the straightforward process which some of Jung's work would seem to indicate; though it must be said in his defence that he does not really pretend that it is. The impact of the unconscious continually brings up personal problems together with the collective imagery, and these two classes of material constantly interact intimately upon each other. Cf. Fordham, 'Notes on the Transference', *New Developments in Analytical Psychology*. London, 1957.

[30] New York, 1916; London, 1917.

[31] Cf. Chap. 7, Part II, 'The Dual Mother Role'.

theoretical statements; he has often said that he only wishes to criticize in so far as Freud claims too general a validity for his theoretical framework, and he claims that he himself uses the technique of psycho-analysis in his practice with suitable patients. He also claims to use Adler's method when he considers it indicated.[32]

1915–THE PRESENT

After the early periods, he gradually ceased to be a specialist, becoming a centre round which not only medical but a number of other specialities could revolve.

His extensive research into mythology convinced him that it was necessary to distinguish a spiritual principle which could not be reduced to anything else; this principle is an opposite to instinct. In his assertion there is no justification for neglect, which is so frequently attributed to him, of the sexual and ego instincts to which Freud and Adler respectively had then given so much attention; indeed, if there were, it would not be possible for the individuation process, the main subject of all Jung's later researches, to take place at all, if only because the transcendent function of the symbol appears only if the opposites be given equal value. The criticism that his postulate has led him to abandon genetic or reductive analysis misses the point: he limits its validity by taking it to be the more important process for the analysis of young people who have difficulties in establishing themselves in the world because their egos fail to mature; but for those whose problems do not come in this class, especially those near-normal people in the latter half of life, for whom life has lost its meaning and purpose, or borderline cases of schizophrenia, or

---

[32] This attitude is possible for Jung because of his work on types, which makes it feasible for him to regard a psychological theory as the expression of a particular predisposition. Inasmuch as people differ from one another there are different ways of dealing with the psyche. Jung includes himself in this relative position. His theories and his method are the expression of his own particular predisposition.

This notion can clearly be misused and is open to all sorts of abuses, but it has the value of avoiding theoretical rigidity. Moreover, Jung has worked out his conclusion in considerable detail, so that his standpoint is fundamentally different from the eclectic position. It is inevitable that he should use psycho-analytic methods in relation to his whole position. It is therefore unlikely that he would use them as a strict Freudian would. The same must apply to Adler's techniques.

some cases of schizophrenia proper, the synthetic approach is the more important.[33]

These considerations throw a feature of the development of Jung's ideas into relief; his position was becoming increasingly relative and he went on to develop instruments, of which the theory of types[34] is a good example, for defining the spheres in which each of the relatively valid methods of investigation can usefully be applied. In principle this position is unexceptionable, his demotion of causality to the status of a relative postulate was revolutionary, for science then operated on the principle that causality was its foundation stone.

In 1917 Jung published 'The Psychology of the Unconscious Processes',[35] which is a summary of his position. In this paper he discusses the causal viewpoint of Freud alongside of Adler's final and teleological theory, conceiving the differences between them in terms of psychological types. He then goes on to elaborate his own position, taking a dream to show the method from which his attitude derived. He analyses the dream in relation to the history of the patient and thus from the causal point of view. This analysis leads him to conclude that a content of the patient's psychology is missing from the environment; only when he investigates the transference is the missing element found—the patient reveals that she experiences Jung as seeming 'sometimes . . . rather dangerous, sinister, like an evil magician. . . .'[36]

It is on the question of how to handle the class of phenomena, collectively termed primordial or archetypal images, of which the

[33] It may seem paradoxical that Jung's contribution should apply particularly to 'normal' people of middle age and to schizophrenics. The difference between the two classes apparently so opposed does not lie, however, in the actual phenomena themselves so much as in the attitude of the consciousness towards them. The 'normal' person has a well-established ego which is able to withstand, and in some degree regulate, the activity of the unconscious. On the contrary, the schizophrenic ego is, to all intents, non-existent, having been replaced by the archetypal images which have as it were, swallowed it up.

[34] Jung's first publication on typology appeared in 1913 and is translated as 'A Contribution to the Study of Psychological Types', in *Collected Papers on Analytical Psychology*. It was delivered to the Psychoanalytic Congress in Munich in 1913.

[35] In *Two Essays on Analytical Psychology* (Collected Works, Vol. VII). London and New York, 1953.

[36] Ibid., p. 89.

magician is an example, that Jung made his new departure. He did not attempt to explain them but instead regarded them as irrational data which could be dealt with adequately only by a new technique which consisted in an act of discrimination, in separating subjective personal from objective psychological facts, of which the magician is a representative. The archetypal image was then investigated on the 'inner' plane. Thus did Jung uncover what he later termed the objective psyche, and in so doing enormously enriched the possibilities of his synthetic method.

There could surely be no better example with which to refute the belief that Jung's discoveries are speculative theories—just the reverse; it was by clearing away a type of theoretical structure, by removing explanations and speculations that he arrived at a new set of phenomena on which his hypotheses of the collective unconscious and the archetypes, so regularly mistaken for rank mysticism, are largely based.

The concepts of the archetypes, the archetypal images, and the collective unconscious have become of such importance for analytical psychology that they need a brief definition here. An archetype is conceived as an unconscious 'X' behind a set of behavioural phenomena of which the primordial image is the most discussed, though not the only representative. There is unfortunately some confusion in terminology here, both in Jung's writings and in those of other analysts, but the distinction between the archetype and its phenomena is essential if confusion is not to follow. The archetypal images have a mythological character, they tend to fascinate, they have 'numen' or mysterious power, and each of them has a positive as well as a negative aspect. Though they appear at times in a discrete form, they merge into each other and so reveal themselves as parts of an essential unity. Jung contends that their content has never been, and probably never will be, exhausted, that is to say, all attempts to raise them to consciousness will inevitably fail, as they have so far done. It will be generally conceded that myths, religions, and folklore are worldwide in their distribution, and that they are collective, group or social phenomena. This fact was one of those which led Jung to call the part of the unconscious from which they emerge the collective unconscious.[37]

[37] These definitions are those to which I adhere. I have elaborated the subject at greater length in 'Biological Theory and the Concept of Arche-

At the same time as his discovery of the first archetypal images, Jung began to elaborate a new method for exploring the collective unconscious which he termed amplification. This is a comparative method by which an obscure fantasy can be thrown into relief by being compared with other, usually mythological, material.[38] In addition he developed introverting techniques of eliciting fantasy material, to which reference is made in more detail later.[39]

The technique of eliciting active fantasies, of which active imagination is a part, resulted in further confirmation of his theoretical position, for he says: 'I can only say that there is probably no motif in any known mythology that does not at some time appear in these configurations.'[40]

The two introverting techniques led to the definition of a development to which Jung gave the name 'individuation', and of which he gave an account in 'The Relation Between the Ego and the Unconscious' (1928).[41]

So far we have considered the unconscious forms alone, but alongside his study of these Jung developed a psychology of consciousness and the conscious mind which is linked with an ego concept derived in part from the association theories of the period, in part from the association experiments. A large number of the associations could be easily elicited and recalled, they were coherent and easily comprehensible, and could be conceived as centring on an organized nucleus—the ego complex.[42] It is important that in *The Psychology of Dementia Praecox* Jung asserts that, since the conscious is linked with perception, the ego must be a

types', *New Developments in Analytical Psychology*. London, 1957. It will be observed that the concept of heredity is not included in my definition; I regard it as unnecessary, in view of the developments in biology since Jung first defined the archetypes.

[38] Jung's use of mythology to throw light on his patients' material has been criticized because it can lead to imposing conclusions on patients. This can, but need not, be the case.   [39] Cf. infra, pp. 67 ff.

[40] 'The Spirit of Psychology', *Spirit and Nature: Papers from the Eranos Yearbooks*. New York, 1954; London, 1955, p. 414.

[41] Cf. *Two Essays on Analytical Psychology* (Collected Works, Vol. VII). London and New York, 1953. For definition and discussion of the individuation process, cf. infra, pp. 49 ff.

[42] The term 'complex' was first introduced by Theodor Ziehen of Berlin. Cf. Jones, *Sigmund Freud, Life and Work*, Vol. II. London and Toronto, 1955, p. 127.

body ego. He says (p. 35): 'The ego is the psychological expression for the firmly associated union of all general bodily sensations.'

The firm unity of the ego runs through all Jung's work, and in the course of years the psychology of the conscious became greatly elaborated and linked up with the notion of attitude. He developed a distinction between the conscious mind and consciousness,[43] the latter being the quality of psychic activity in the sense that the activity can be perceived. The conscious mind, however, refers to a class of psychic activities having the capacity to reach clear definition in consciousness and therefore which are also capable of being manipulated plastically. They can be in the field of consciousness or they can be unconscious, and, when repressed, cannot reach the condition of consciousness. It would therefore be logical if these repressed contents were referred to as the repressed conscious, and not the repressed unconscious, as is usually done. The functions and attitudes of the types make up the main contents of the conscious mind as a whole, which can therefore be completely defined only when no part of them is repressed.

It has already been noted that in 'The Psychology of the Unconscious Processes' Jung developed his view of psychological types and used it to account for the divergences of viewpoint in psycho-analysis. His theory[44] is a flexible and complex system, but it is essentially a theory of conscious processes though, at the same time, it is related to his whole view of the unconscious and to the process of individuation. There is no introverted conscious mind without an extraverted unconscious, no extraverted conscious without an introverted unconscious, and so, within wide limits, the type can be modified by raising the 'counter-type' to consciousness; while through the symbolic realization of the self, the two opposing tendencies, on the one hand the conscious mind and on the other the unconscious, on the one hand introversion and on the other extraversion, can be brought into reasonable harmony.[45] Each type, therefore, represents a one-

---

[43] The German word 'bewusstheit' is translated in the Collected Works as 'conscious' or 'conscious mind'; 'Bewusstsein' is translated as 'consciousness. This distinction is clarified in the Collected Works, though Jung himself uses the term 'bewusstsein' in the sense of conscious mind or consciousness.   [44] *Psychological Types.* London, 1923.

[45] Exactly the same applies to the theory of 'function types', of which there are two pairs: two rational, thinking and feeling; two irrational, sensation and intuition.

sided picture of the whole psychic organism. It is a picture of the conscious mind.

Jung's large book, *Psychological Types* (1921), is more than its title suggests; it marks a further development of his effort to relate clinical researches to other of the various disciplines sometimes called the humanities.[46] In it he applies the theory of types to religious controversy, philosophy, aesthetics, psychiatry, history, etc. Of special interest is his work on the psychological processes behind the development of Christianity, his comparison of Christianity with some aspects of Oriental religions, and his welding of these together, using the images in Spitteler's *Prometheus and Epimetheus* as a basis for his interpretation. The book is one that repays close attention; here we can discover Jung as the interpreter of history and of human thought and feeling; here is the basis for a new orientation, not only towards normal psychology and psychopathology,[47] but also towards civilization as a whole. It is informed scientific speculation opening up new fields for investigation.

In the chapter entitled 'The Problem of Types in Poetry' is a long discussion of the reconciling symbol, the *self*. If we turn back to the 1902 case it will be found that the patient became introverted during the period of her 'revelations' and yet she subsequently adapted as an extraverted personality. The introverted development culminated in the production of a mandala, and though Jung did not then know it, this was an image of what he later termed the *self*, an inner principle of order foreshadowing the later integration of the patient's complexes into a working unity.

When Jung recommended his patients to study the processes going on within themselves by employing active imagination he found mandalas were a regular feature of their pictures; these seemed to appear when the final synthesis between the conscious and unconscious processes began to take place. Starting to observe them in 1916, he watched their development and also

[46] As a book *Psychological Types* is much clearer than *The Psychology of the Unconscious*, which began the process though in a different way.

[47] Comparatively little is said on this topic in the volume but in the description of the types each section contains a statement of the pathological symptoms each type is likely to produce. Elsewhere Jung remarks that his theory of types grew out of the problem of which direction regression was likely to take if the conscious attitude failed.

discovered that they occurred in mediaeval Christian mysticism. He then met Richard Wilhelm,[48] and the two found common ground; mandala images were part of it. Starting from different viewpoints, their lines of research met; the result was a book, *The Secret of the Golden Flower*,[49] first published in 1929. In this work Wilhelm translated a Taoist text describing the process of development which results from meditation, and Jung contributed a psychological commentary showing how Chinese mysticism can be approached with the aid of analytical psychology, and how the imagery occurs in the East just as much as in the West, though the conscious attitude from which it is viewed is radically different. This Jung attributes to cultural factors. The East, he says, starts its meditation techniques from a balance of intuitively apprehended opposites, Yang and Yin, from which man frees himself through a process of inner growth analogous to but not identical with our individuation. On the contrary, the West starts from a one-sided position, it starts from a conscious attitude which has as its best tool the scientific intellect. In order to approach the position of the East, Western man cannot abandon his science without suffering a serious loss and, in consequence, he cannot take over the Eastern standpoint without applying his scientific instrument to the task. It is Jung's achievement that he succeeded in bringing Eastern mysticism and Western science closer together: he finds that if science is used to study the psyche, we arrive at the position of conflict between the opposites comprising spirit and instinct. If we are able to balance these and maintain an equilibrium, a synthesis gradually occurs. It is the synthetic process which is the same in the East as in the West.

The methods which culminated in *Psychological Types* and *The Secret of the Golden Flower* are repeated over and over again

[48] Richard Wilhelm was a sinologist who went to China as a Christian missionary. He was, however, so much impressed by Chinese philosophy that he gave up his missionary purpose and made a detailed study of Chinese religions. He wrote a history of the Chinese people and made several translations of Chinese texts and books. The most famous of these is perhaps his translation of the *I Ching* (London, 2 vols., 1951).

[49] English edition, London, 1931. Jung appears to have been concerned lest, if he published these pictures too early, their magical effect would lead to the invalidation of many of those subsequently produced by his patients.

in different spheres. Jung starts in each case from clinical material and finds new territories opening before him. Just as he gained access to Oriental philosophy from his observations in Zurich, so also did he gain an understanding of Gnosticism, early and mediaeval Christianity,[50] alchemy,[51] Yoga,[52] and each time he kept to his scientific roots, though there was not always a Wilhelm to spring up as a collaborator. By extending his clinical findings to the general field of human experience, Jung increased the significance of his work.

The intimate relationship between the phenomena he observed in his patients and the myths of civilization leads to four kinds of knowledge which are closely inter-related. In the first place it leads to a knowledge about the nature of symbolical experience,[53] in the second it investigates the antecedents of individuation and in so doing demonstrates the generality of the symbolic development essential for its realization, in the third place it gives material which will help in understanding the historical development of consciousness, and so leads to the fourth kind of knowledge, the speculative evaluation of essentially modern problems.

Jung's astonishing ability to orientate himself amongst the mass of material derives in a large measure from the concept of history. 'Without the historical connection, they [his psychological observations] would remain suspended in mid-air, a mere curiosity.'[54] By reviewing his material in relation to history he has arrived at the conclusion that the main problem of our era is spiritual (or, more accurately, psychological); he bases this partly on the historical argument that the age-old projections of the archetypal images have been progressively withdrawn because the discoveries of the natural sciences have proved their irrelevance

[50] Cf. *Aion* (Collected Works, Vol. IX, Part II). London and New York, 1958.

[51] Cf. *Psychology and Alchemy* (Collected Works, Vol. XII). London and New York, 1953; *Mysterium Coniunctionis*, Zurich, 1955, et al.

[52] Cf. Essays in *Psychology and Religion: West and East* (Collected Works, Vol. XI). London and New York, 1958.

[53] Cf. my 'Reflections on Image and Symbol', *New Developments in Analytical Psychology*, London, 1957, for a discussion of Jung's theory of symbolic forms.

[54] *Psychology and Religion: West and East* (Collected Works, Vol. XI). London and New York, 1958, p. 102.

in the physical world. Psychology has continued the analysis of the old projection systems such as alchemy,[55] and has gone further to reveal the projections which individuals and groups make on each other.

As a result all the psychic energy which flowed into the projections has not been lost, but has been freed to appear from its true, though previously unrealized, source within the individual, disturbing the conscious mind if it tries to meet the afflux of libido with an inadequate attitude. From this arises consciousness of innumerable problems which are expressed in the individual sphere as neuroses, psychoses, and personal problems; in the collective sphere in the deification of leaders, wars, economic depressions, and so forth.[56]

Since these conclusions are not based upon historical research alone, but are linked up with contemporary processes through the material produced by patients, it becomes apparent that there are avowed patients, and countless others, who live as if they were still, for instance, living in the Middle Ages, or whose psychology belongs to early or even pre-Christian times. Jung has shown that the psychic life of many people now living is by no means contemporary but corresponds to many earlier phases of human development. The past is alive in the present; to this the Nazi and Fascist movements have recently given eloquent testimony and contemporary events show a scarcely less barbaric pattern. Jung's speculation thus appears to have alarming confirmation in being a piece of living history.

But 'modern man', according to Jung's definition, is different: he has torn himself away from the unconscious and is isolated, standing between the past and the future which he consequently approaches without prejudice:

[55] When this paper was originally written *Psychology and Alchemy* had not been translated. To have inserted a review of these researches would have expanded this essay too greatly. The reader is referred to the following: *Psychology and Alchemy* (Collected Works, Vol. XII). London and New York, 1953. 'The Psychology of the Transference', *The Practice of Psychotherapy* (Collected Works, Vol. XVI). London and New York, 1954. *Aion* (Collected Works, Vol. IX, Part II). London and New York, 1958. *Mysterium Coniunctionis*, Zurich, 1955.

[56] This argument does not depend upon whether these events are more or less frequent than they were before. It explains why man now tends to believe that he is the cause of them.

... he has become 'unhistorical' in the deepest sense and has estranged himself from the mass of men who live entirely within the bounds of tradition. Indeed, he is completely modern only when he has come to the very edge of the world, leaving behind him all that has been discarded and outgrown and acknowledging that he stands before a void out of which all things may grow. [57] ... To me (Jung continues) the crux of the spiritual problem of today is to be found in the fascination which psychic life exerts upon modern man. If we are pessimists, we shall call it a sign of decadence; if we are optimistically inclined, we shall see in it the promise of a far-reaching spiritual change in the Western world. [58]

Clearly Jung believes that analytical psychology is in a position to foster a development of far-reaching individual and social significance.

Modern psychological development, he says, leads to a much better understanding as to what man really consists of. The gods at first lived in superhuman power and beauty on the top of snow-clad mountains or in the darkness of caves, woods, and seas. Later on they drew together into one god, and then that god became man. But in our day even the God-man seems to have descended from his throne and to be dissolving himself in the common man. That is probably why his seat is empty. [59]

In a sense we are confronted with the same old religious problem, but in a different guise.

Religious experience is absolute; it cannot be disputed. You can only say that you have never had such an experience, whereupon your opponent will reply: 'Sorry, I have.' And there your discussion will come to an end. [60]

This is distasteful to those who like to discuss everything, and it is uncongenial to rationalists.

The final experience of the individuation process, which is to be conceived as the culmination of a long historical development, is likewise overwhelming; it cannot be refuted, but it can be studied. We are beginning to know something about it, but empirically it is a final and conclusive statement in which the psychic energy moves from the ego to a non-ego centre, depicted

[57] 'The Spiritual Problem of Modern Man', *Modern Man in Search of a Soul*. London, 1933, p. 228.

[58] Ibid., p. 251.

[59] 'Psychology and Religion', in *Psychology and Religion: West and East* (Collected Works, Vol. XI). London and New York, 1958, p. 84.

[60] Ibid., pp. 104-5.

in the 'centre' of the mandalas of Jung's patients. In historical mandalas there is always a god, in the modern ones there is none; in Jung's early case the centre contained a 'spiritual force', in his later ones a diamond or other symbol emphasizes its importance. The absence of a god is interpreted to mean that the centring process refers to the personality; it is an intuition of the possibility of being whole or points symbolically to the direction in which wholeness lies. The interpretation as well as the significant difference in symbolic form is modern.

Jung's contribution towards the postulated spiritual crisis is, therefore, to provide a means of experiencing spiritual 'numina' as facts so that they cannot be denied and at the same time their experience need not offend the rational intellect, whose activity is enhanced and directed into a new and positive channel by a change in its use. He turns it inwards, using it as a tool with which to study the inner world of primordial images as they emerge from the collective unconscious: this is how he has attempted to treat spiritual values by empirical scientific methods.

For many of us his method has not only solved an intellectual quandary, it has also circumvented a danger: in approaching the objective psyche we risk being destroyed by it, and indeed we cannot help a considerable destruction of supposedly well-established values. If we have no dogma and no solution, what is there to help us through the crisis except the objective and impartial scientific standpoint? In practice it is the attitude of empirical science which provides the check and avoids the psychotic-like disintegration which threatens those who, like Jung's modern man, stand before a void containing the titanic forces of the unconscious.

The emergence of the *self* presents us with a paradox; if we try to grasp what happens when the conscious functions, of which the objective scientific intelligence is the main representative, fuse with the unconscious functions, the archetypes, we get something which is at once science and religion but which is at the same time neither the one nor the other. It contains the essential core of Jung's work to which it gives extraordinary and fascinating originality because it is revealed as depending ultimately upon a symbol.[61]

[61] Cf. Fordham, 'Reflections on Image and Symbol', *New Developments in Analytical Psychology*. London, 1957.

It is at this point that Jung might have become a mystic, or gone off into metaphysical speculation. Both of these alternatives he rejects when he says:

I trust I have given no cause for the misunderstanding that I know anything about the nature of the 'centre'—for it is simply unknowable and can only be expressed symbolically through its own phenomenology, as is the case, incidentally, with every object of experience.[62]

THE STATUS OF JUNG'S RESEARCHES

The fact that Jung regards the principle of causality as holding a relative position in the totality of the psyche,[63] as well as the problematic nature of the self and his much-advertised though little-understood interest in occultism, has given rise to the question whether his work can be regarded as scientific. Those who believe it is not try to find some other category into which they can fit his labours. He must be either a mystic or a philosopher. The subject of mysticism and religion will be taken up later;[64] only a short statement is necessary here. The issue appears to turn on frames of reference: to Jung the phenomena of mysticism are expressions of the collective unconscious and consequently take a relative position within the totality of psychic functions; his whole conception of mysticism is psychological and relative. Mystics, on the other hand, usually assert that their experiences are of absolute transcendental realities and even essentially different from any experiences encountered in such a psychological process as individuation.[65]

The question whether Jung is a philosopher is in one sense scarcely less difficult to answer. There can be little doubt that contemporary philosophers reject him out of hand. Individuation is, however, bound up with forming an individual philosophy of life. It is not explicitly so defined by Jung, but one of its salient features is, in my view, the gradual formation of a

[62] *Psychology and Alchemy* (Collected Works, Vol. XII). London and New York, 1953, p. 208.

[63] Cf. particularly his concept of synchronicity, 'Synchronicity: An Acausal Connecting Principle', in C. G. Jung and W. Pauli, *The Interpretation of Nature and the Psyche*. London and New York, 1955.

[64] Cf. pp. 113 ff. and pp. 130 ff. below.

[65] Cf. p. 147 below.

relatively stable attitude by the whole man to his whole life.[66] Jung says of a philosophy of life:[67]

As the most complex of psychic structures, a man's philosophy of life forms the counterpole to the physiologically conditioned psyche, and, as the highest psychic dominant it ultimately determines the latter's fate. It guides the life of the therapist and shapes the spirit of his therapy. Since it is an essentially subjective system, despite the most rigorous objectivity, it may, and very likely will, be shattered time after time in colliding with the truth of the patient, but it rises again, rejuvenated by the experience. Conviction easily turns into self-defence and is seduced into rigidity, and this is inimical to life. The test of a firm conviction is its elasticity and flexibility; like every other exalted truth, it thrives best on the admission of its errors.[68]

Further he goes on to say:

I can hardly draw a veil over the fact that we psychotherapists ought really to be philosophers or philosophic doctors—or rather that we already are so, though we are unwilling to admit it because of the glaring contrast between our work and what passes for philosophy in the universities. We could also call it religion *in statu nascendi*, for in the vast confusion that reigns at the roots of life there is no line of division between philosophy and religion. Nor does the unrelieved strain of the psychotherapeutic situation, with its host of impressions and emotional disturbances, leave us much leisure for the systematization of thought. Thus we have no clear exposition of guiding principles drawn from life to offer either to the philosophers or to the theologians.[69]

Inasmuch as Jung is a psychotherapist it may be assumed that he has formed a philosophy of life as here defined.

Not being a philosopher myself, I must conclude by adding Jung's view:

Psychology takes the psyche for its subject-matter, and philosophy— to put it briefly—takes the world. . . . Neither discipline can do without the other, and the one always furnishes the implicit—and frequently even unconscious—primary assumptions of the other.[70]

[66] Cf. also pp. 49ff. below.
[67] The German word *Weltanschauung* is the term Jung uses.
[68] 'Psychotherapy and a Philosophy of Life'. *The Practice of Psychotherapy* (Collected Works, Vol. XVI). London and New York, 1954, p. 79.
[69] Ibid.
[70] 'The Basic Postulates of Analytical Psychology'. *Modern Man in Search of a Soul*. London, 1933, p. 207.

We may now turn to the claim of analytical psychology to be a science. If it does not rise to the precision of the exact natural sciences and is sometimes classed as one of the human sciences, this is because of the general problem presented by psychology as a whole. Is it or is it not true that human beings are dreadfully irrational? Is not the psyche at once the subject and object of study? It is these questions which have to be answered in connection with a definition of what is meant by 'science', a word whose meaning is by no means stable. Analytical psychology aims at discovering how the psyche works and accumulates records which can be subjected to a comparative study and theoretical treatment.[71] This comparative study can extend to philosophies of life as well, it stops short only where the whole man is integrated.

Without doubt Jung's positive estimation of higher spiritual values has made scientists doubt his credentials and causes many of them to fear that he is somehow smuggling in non-scientific material. His early work is usually recognized for some reason as beyond criticism, but his later researches, the real mark of his genius, are too often smirched by much faint-heartedness. Spiritual values are irreducible functions of the psyche, that is Jung's contention; viewed as facts no scientist can fail to take them into account without betraying his calling, even if they be too arbitrary in their functioning for logical treatment. This has been recognized by Jung just as much as by his critics; he devised his comparative method to meet just this difficulty. The reproach of smuggling in non-rational facts in rational guise is beside the point.

It is often said that Jung speculates; why not, pray? Is not this

R. Hostie (*Religion and the Psychology of Jung*. London and New York, 1957) and Victor White (*God and the Unconscious*. London, 1952) both agree that from the Catholic position Jung does not show much sign of fitting into Roman philosophy. It may here be added that Hostie consistently accepts Jung as a scientist. As, however, he wishes to separate psychology and theology, with a view to discrediting most of what Jung means, one can scarcely feel much confidence in his motivation.

[71] Woodger, in his excellent essay *Physics, Psychology and Medicine* (Cambridge, 1957), bases his argument on the following three requirements of science: bright ideas, observations, and apparatus. The bright ideas must be related to the observations but can reach from inspiration to logically constructed explanatory theories and mathematics; the apparatus can be anything from a notebook to atom splitting machines.

a necessary part of science? To do so would be illegitimate only if the facts were not distinguished from the speculations and theories. Jung is a prodigious collector of facts and theories; both are essential parts of the scientific discipline.

The best basis for the criticism that he is unscientific is the methods of investigation Jung employs. These cannot be put in their proper perspective without going back to the beginning, for right from the start Jung realized the weak point of his experimental technique. He understood that the sex and personality of the investigator influenced the test result to an unspecified extent;[72] the tendency to exclude this early work from criticism because subjective personality factors were unimportant, puts Jung's critics fifty years behind him in their estimation of his research.

The next step made the personality of the investigator not less but more important. The use of free association to confirm test interpretations was valid enough to be accepted, though under protest from some; the use of interpretations to overcome postulated resistances with a view to stimulating the emergence of ideas from the postulated unconscious psyche produced a chorus of often abusive criticism, still very much alive today. It is true that when the experimental framework was relaxed and replaced by free associations, combined with interpretations, in fact with psycho-analysis, the whole field of operations clearly became vastly more complex; the analyst could not hope to be free from error due to the intrusion of his own personality. Classical science has always sought to eliminate this, and the criticism of subjectivity needs the closest consideration. It may be remarked, however, that if analysts had been discouraged, their whole investigation would have had to cease. Another alternative however presented itself: the subjective factor could be taken as part of the whole procedure.

This is exactly what Jung did when he decided to take the personality of the experimenter, and later of the analyst, fully into account by proposing the analysis of the analyst. Attempts were made to uncover the source of personal bias by analysing the analysts before they started investigating the unconscious of patients. Though it was a very substantial advance, this develop-

[72] Cf. Baynes, 'Freud versus Jung', *Analytical Psychology and the English Mind*. London, 1950, p. 108.

ment was only partially successful. It did not, according to Jung at least, eliminate the influence of the analyst's personality, it only revealed its extent; his own personality came to be seen as very much more part of an analyst's descriptions than was assumed to be the case in the physical or natural sciences. The question whether the analyst's personality need be a source of error was not then considered seriously; only later did it seem likely to turn into an asset.

Without coming to any conclusion about the validity of their method, analysts continued to study the associations produced by patients. As this proceeded, it became clear that imagination played a large part in them. So-called memories came to light; some of them could be confirmed, but many could not, and were highly fantastic and improbable. Jung, as we have seen, became particularly interested in these 'memories', and in agreement with Freud he held that they were not memories at all but fantasies—fantasies which had the same psychological reality as memories. But as we have also seen Jung went further than Freud; he concluded that in the unconscious there must be special archetypal determinants. These he confirmed by the following technique:

I . . . took up a dream image or an association of the patient's and, with this as a point of departure, set him the task of elaborating or developing his theme by giving free rein to his fantasy.[73]

It is most important to realize firstly that archetypal images are general: they occur everywhere; secondly that, because they are psychologically objective, they can evidently be considered as the correlate of matter in other natural sciences. The concept of the objectivity of the archetypal forms was methodologically crucial. It led to changes in analytic techniques and to the realization that when the analyst meets his patient in a transference, and then describes the archetypal forms arising in the patient, he becomes part of these phenomena, no longer in a subjective but in an objective sense, the archetypes in the patient being the same as those in the analyst—the only difference being individual variations in the form of their expression. The theory of archetypes thus gives a new basis for the analyst's earlier realization that he is part of his descriptive accounts, but he need

[73] 'The Spirit of Psychology', *Spirit and Nature*, p. 412.

no longer fear so much the reproach of subjective error which is theoretically eliminated. Ideally it means that, at the archetypal level, an analyst cannot go wrong if sufficiently analysed.[74]

This theory has been extended to science as a whole by the Swiss physicist Professor Pauli, who has pointed out the relevance of the idea of archetypes for the theory of scientific knowledge; he has suggested that natural scientists are not different from psychologists in being outside their description, though the objects to be described fall into a different class. Pauli says that '. . . many physicists have recently emphasized anew that intuition and the direction of attention play a considerable role in the development of concepts.'[75] He goes on to contend that up to now there has been no means of defining the relation between the order perceived in nature through sense data and the theoretical formulations within the psyche. And then he says:

> As *ordering* operators and image-formers . . . the archetypes . . . function as the sought-for bridge between sense perception and the ideas and are, accordingly, a necessary presupposition even for evolving a scientific theory of nature.[76]

Jung's thesis changes a concept of science which has never corresponded to the experience of scientists. The supposedly cold intellectual exercise which has led to the erection of more and more expensive and more and more complicated pieces of apparatus, always an illusion, is changed to a new one: science becomes a discipline in which both the intellect and the apparatus are the end products of a more emotional and elementary process represented by the dynamic, affective archetypal forms.

[74] Analysts only live approximately up to this criterion because their psyches are not constructed of archetypes alone. In the *Psychology of the Unconscious*, London, 1917 (p. 232) Jung first showed the relation of scientific theory to mythology. He takes two of Freud's theories and traces the mythological parallels to them. He does the same with his own theory of psychical energy in 'On Psychical Energy', (*On Psychic Energy* (Collected Works, Vol. VIII), London and New York, 1959), while in *Two Essays on Analytical Psychology* (Collected Works, Vol. VII), London and New York, 1953, he shows (pp. 66 f.) that Mayer's concept of the conservation of energy has extraordinarily primitive roots.

[75] 'The Influence of Archetypal Ideas on the Scientific Theories of Kepler', in C. G. Jung and W. Pauli, *The Interpretation of Nature and the Psyche*. London and New York, 1955, p. 151.

[76] Op. cit., p. 153.

Scientists have always engaged in controversies and displayed considerable heat in them; by way of illustration it may be remarked that in my own lifetime there have been vigorous and not very rational public discussions in biology and physiology, not to mention the conflicts which have reft the various schools of dynamic psychology. But all these have previously been viewed as by-products not belonging to the essence of science. The view that archetypes lie at the root of scientific discovery puts these conflicts in a very different light; it means that they are to be considered part of the whole process of discovery.

Professor Polanyi has recently taken up a comparable position. He says: 'The outbreak of emotions in the course of discovery is well known';[77] and he gives many striking instances. Then he continues:

Science is regarded as objectively established in spite of its passionate origins . . . but . . . I do actually want to show that scientific passions are no mere psychological by-play, but have a logical function which contributes an indispensable element to science.[78]

One may object to Polanyi's use of the term psychological, but if the essential idea be correct, it follows that analytical psychology is not only scientific but a basic science because it can reveal the nature of the natural sciences themselves.

[77] 'Passion and Controversy in Science', *Lancet*, Vol. I, 1956, p. 921.
[78] Ibid.

III

THE CONCEPT OF THE OBJECTIVE
PSYCHE[1]

THE concept of the 'objective psyche' was first introduced by Jung[2] some years ago in order to cover the field of research which he had previously defined as the collective unconscious. It is to be preferred for our present purpose in that it includes the individuality; moreover it defines the quality of experience in a more rich and definite way than the term 'collective unconscious' though it also refers to those psychic contents which cannot be seen as part of oneself as a known subject. They always have been and still are *only seen objectively*, i.e. they are separate from oneself (the subject) and are different in nature from the whole idea anyone has, or indeed can have or could have, of himself as an ego. In consequence they have usually been experienced as cosmic.

The objective psyche was and is still conceived and experienced as different in nature from the ego as a conscious subjective function. It has given rise to all sorts of religions, culture patterns, scientific theories and illusions. It seems inevitably to project itself, or rather, it is found projected. Looking back historically, it seems as if it has been almost literally living its own life in the stars as astrology, in matter as alchemy, in mountains, trees, groves, in heaven, in hell, and only within the tiny span of rather more than half a century has it become a subject-matter for psychology as if there were nowhere else for it to go; here it appears in interpersonal relations where it is mistakenly understood personalistically or in mass psychoses where it can be seen in political philosophies or quasi-religious wars. It is only through

[1] Presidential address, delivered to the Medical Section of the British Psychological Society and published in the *British Journal of Medical Psychology*, Vol. XXIV, Part 4, 1951, pp. 221–31.

[2] 'The Development of Personality', *The Development of Personality* (Collected Works, Vol. XVII). London and New York, 1954, pp. 167 ff.

psychological understanding that it can be brought into relation with man. Psychological method is, however, the instrument which could never achieve its integration without the fact of individuality which separates each man from his fellow, and this leads to the possibility of its being integrated. In doing so it does not become less objective, it becomes a psychological object—a 'presentation', as the late Dr. H. G. Baynes put it in his paper 'The unconscious as the real object of psychology.'[3]

Why I have preferred the term objective psyche will, I hope, become even more clear as we proceed. I might have spoken of the psychology of the masses, for anthropological and biological concepts will be introduced for comparative purposes, but I wanted to include the self in the centre of this discussion.

Social anthropology has made us familiar with the notion of *culture patterns* in civilization. These man has gradually developed throughout the ages so that they come to determine the behaviour and beliefs of the members of any particular group.

Ruth Benedict[4] pointed this out when she said:

No man ever looks at the world with pristine eyes. He sees it edited by a definite set of customs and institutions and ways of thinking. Even in his philosophical probings, . . . his very concepts of the true and the false will still have reference to his particular traditional custom. The life history of the individual is first and foremost an accommodation to the patterns and standards traditionally handed down in his community. From the moment of his birth the customs into which he is born shape his experience and behaviour.

This concept is static.

Anthropologists have, however, needed to develop other concepts to account for the spread of cultures; as, for instance, that contained in Professor Kroeber's Huxley Memorial Lecture for 1945 on 'The ancient oïkumenê as an historic culture aggregate.'[5] In this he compares the spread of culture to

. . . a spark somehow falling on a textile, slowly smouldering and finally enlarging its way through a fabric, the greater intensity of combustion being always where the flame has reached only just lately; until the spatial frame of the cultural web is reached, so to speak with the oceans.

[3] In *Analytical Psychology and the English Mind*. London, 1950.

[4] *Patterns of Culture*. London, 1940, p. 2.

[5] *Journal of the Royal Anthropological Institute*, Vol. LXXI, Parts 1-2, 1945, p. 10.

Is this so different from Jung's idea of the cultural activity of an archetype? I am not sure that he has put it so explicitly, but I will formulate it as follows. Assuming that the conscious standards of a particular culture begin to wear thin, there start all sorts of cults and new ideas which reach out towards an adequate formulation for the activity of the collective unconscious, whose activity increases because the psychic energy previously bound in the traditions becomes liberated. Then these 'sparks' coalesce through a single figure, sometimes a real person, sometimes a mythological figure, who inspired men already prepared for it by the trends present in the thought and values of the period. From this springs a new cultural impulse. Western civilization began in this way, and our contemporary condition is in many respects similar to the state of affairs before Christianity made itself felt in the midst of the Roman Empire whose foundations were shaking.

Both the anthropological ideas take account of a seemingly objective process, two aspects of which appear and can be compared profitably to the collective conscious (the culture pattern) and the collective unconscious (the oikumenê). They each imply an object which acts on men and women, and there is no room for the individual as the source in these patterns or dynamisms.

Turning to the biological field, Professor J. Z. Young has chosen for his Reith Lectures[6] the field of brain anatomy and physiology. He presents many ideas which to one with a training in analytical psychology are congenial. For instance, he elaborates the idea of brain models, the patterns and images of the real world which we laboriously construct and which apparently cannot be regarded simply as the mirror image of an external reality at all. These are then integrated more and more till we get the complex brain activity which we have termed mind. The nuclei of activity co-ordinating on the basis of a whole brain may one day bring the archetypes within the range of experimental study. Next, Professor Young includes the idea of random areas of brain function, which he thinks are significant because through it new nuclei of organization can be formed. The idea that seemingly arbitrary events tend to group themselves in a significant way,[7]

[6] *The Listener*, 21 December 1950, p. 780.
[7] Cf. Jung, 'Archaic Man', *Modern Man in Search of a Soul*. London, 1933. Also 'Introduction' to the *I Ching* (trans. Wilhelm-Baynes). London and New York, 1950.

and that this grouping is related to the psychical nuclei in the unconscious, termed archetypes, would correspond to the coalescence of random brain activity and the formation of partially organized brain models. Further, the evolutionary notion of continuity falls into line with the conception of the collective unconscious, and finally Professor Young, in a quotation from Proust, even wants us to consider ourselves not so much as a single entity but as many interacting ones. The quotation from Proust runs:

I was not one man only, but the steady parade hour after hour of an army in close formation, in which there appeared according to the moment impassioned men, jealous men no two of whom were jealous of the same woman.

Without putting this forward as a precise definition of what is meant by the objective psyche, I think the necessary reflective observation has been made in this quotation. I reproduce it because it illustrates how purely biological thinking is able to arrive independently at an idea of regarding whole areas or parts of ourselves objectively.

It is impossible not to think of our subject without considering the psycho-analytic theory of object relations. According to this theory the psyche is built up through the introjection of good and bad objects. Where it differs from the concept here employed is in the fact that rather more emphasis is given to the original psychic nature of the object. Thus, if I have understood it correctly the object relation theory postulates an external object which itself shapes the form libido takes before it is introjected. On the other hand, I assert that the libido is predisposed to adhere to certain objects. Thus in the infant's relation to the breast he is inherently predisposed to form an image of the breast and no other—*not*, for instance, a *jabberwock*. This idea seems to be obvious. Winnicott[8] in his presidential address to the Medical Section of the British Psychological Society expressed graphically and even dramatically rather more than I am asserting. I refer to the passage on the infant's capacity for hallucinating a breast apparently before he experiences the breast his mother actually offers him. While I would not regard this as impossible, I do not know how to find out whether it is true or not. I therefore prefer to adhere to the more cautious formulation enunciated above.

[8] 'Pediatrics and Psychiatry', *British Journal of Medical Psychology*, Vol. XXI, Part 4, 1948, p. 229.

Jung's conception of the objective psyche was arrived at through the study of psychiatric disorders. Early in his researches he was struck by the difficulty of understanding the psychotic process, and we have not got much further in our grasp of the matter—neither the patient nor the doctor is really able to understand it, though both are all too ready to produce explanations.

I want to underline the idea that many schizophrenics are the victims of psychic objectivity. Hallucinations and delusions are experienced as objectively as we experience similar and sometimes identical phenomena in dreams, and as mystics have experienced and still do experience them in waking states.

It should perhaps be stated here, in order to make clear what I mean, that many of the phenomena of schizophrenia have in themselves nothing to do with an illness because they are released from the unconscious. The phenomena are only 'distributed' differently from the normal—or to put it another way, the capacity to communicate intelligibly to an ordinary man is disturbed.

A schizophrenic woman asked a policeman to communicate with me from the police station to which she had been taken. The policeman told me that she had been brought in for obstructing the traffic, but the woman gave a very different story. She said she had been making figures of eight in the middle of the road; she had kept to her track with precision and the stupid taxi-drivers had nearly run her down.

I pointed out to her that the taxi-drivers could not be expected to know that she was drawing their attention to eternal values by acting out the symbol of eternity, the 8, before them in a place they could not fail to notice. I was bound to reflect, however, that if the same area as that covered by the schizophrenic had been marked off with red flags, the known signs of danger, in the place of a harmless lady, no taxi-driver in his senses would drive over that area. It was a problem of culture pattern and brain model.

Quite recently a patient whose interviews had been largely dominated by persecutors who caused her very great distress, came to the interview a changed person. During the hour she looked up at a picture on the wall and remarked that it was a new one. But in fact it was not so; she simply saw a different picture. It was clear that an important part of herself had, almost literally, been in the picture on the wall; now that she had become her true self the projection could be withdrawn and the picture became to her the one I saw. The woman saw the picture objectively before and after the change in herself, only she saw a different image. This event occurred within the analysis and within the transference where I had been one of her persecutors and the cause of her distress.

This illustrates a point about the transference phenomena to support my thesis. If the analyst is not present, there is no real personal object, and the real objectivity of the psyche as 'another person' cannot be grasped in substance—it can only be conceived or imagined. The patient can make a fantasy or an idea about the object, but this is not sufficient to move him deeply. It is only when a real person, the analyst, becomes the real object, in other words, *when the 'hallucination' becomes true*, that we get the measure of objective reality of which I am speaking.

If we suppose there are psychical phenomena which can be classed as objective and because of this can usually be seen only in projection, is there a means by which we can study the objects? Assume that a psychotic is correct in many of the things he says, only that he cannot handle them appropriately. Can we then achieve his kind of objectivity not only in the transference but also more specifically in relation to ourselves?

It was with the aim of testing this that Jung used active imagination. The term means that suspending our current presuppositions, conscious and established models of thought, feeling or extraverted perception, we allow images to become active—to treat them as if they were different but real persons to whom we give form and react to. In some ways the terms meditation or contemplation are more appropriate. Joanna Field[9] used 'contemplative action' for the same process. My objection to this is that both terms have been used in mysticism, and contemplation in particular is concerned with the absence of an object—not at all the case in active imagination. However, so long as this is understood contemplation seems a good word to express the subjective end of the procedure. One might well develop this line of thought by saying that the subject can be passive (observing) or active (reflecting, drawing conclusions, or, more primitively, taking part in the activity of the image or images).

[9] *On Not Being Able to Paint*. London, 1950.

37

The conclusion drawn from the experiences of a growing number of people who have used active imagination confirms the notion that certain contents of the personality are peculiarly difficult to assimilate, i.e. understand and control, and, indeed, that they can never be controlled by the ego, in as much as it is the centre of a conscious being. In assessing this material it must be admitted that relatively few people have so far used the method, and there are many analyses conducted on Jungian lines where it does not occur and where dreams or transference phenomena can be seen to fulfil the same function.

It must be admitted, however, that the kind of person who can employ active imagination is important. There are those who like to think of these persons in terms of psychopathology, but I prefer to put it in terms of types, since it is evident that many of those who can appreciate the objective psyche through active imagination do not come within the range of psychiatric abnormality. A certain capacity for introverted perception is necessary; it can be developed in analysis, but not always sufficiently. The two perceptive functions, intuition and sensation, can be used with equal effect, though the quality of reality is given more by sensation which it seems needs a real object through which to perceive the image. The woman who saw the image of herself in the picture did so by means of introverted sensation; she needed the picture in order to see herself. Intuition needs no object—as if by magic or revelation a whole train of images can emerge from nowhere. The introverted intuitive is hard to analyse because directly any difficulty is to be met a stream of ways out is invented.

There are, I think, enough examples to hazard general statements, but further evidence is necessary to increase the probability of any view we may formulate. We require a way of interdigitating our findings with comparable phenomena in space and time. This way is the comparative method of amplification. By comparing the products of active imagination with similar material from past and present we can bring all kinds of parallels to bear upon our observations to see history and contemporary events in a kind of psychological test-tube. This subject is therefore important enough to be discussed, even though it will take us somewhat off our main line of argument.

The method is one which springs from a spontaneous tendency

in human beings. Whenever an incomprehensible event takes place an attempt is made to understand it in terms of what is already known. For instance, an incomprehensible feeling inside the chest or abdomen is sometimes said to be 'cancer' or 'tuberculosis' or something of that sort. If it be in the brain or felt to be in the mind the term used may be 'insane', 'mad', or 'schizophrenic'. These words give a certain measure of understanding to the experience—they are amplifications, which can usually be analysed out, reduced, and replaced by more adequate and useful formulations. The understanding of them can be deepened and related to the internal and external life of the person concerned. The amplification at this level is, in other words, simply the first step in knowing more about oneself.

Amplifications can occur at many levels and are made for many reasons. Jung has pointed out that the study of dream series reveals amplification. The dream images revolve round and round a central core which is at first referred to and then gradually becomes more and more in evidence till it may, but does not always, appear with full clarity.

As a method, amplification is different. Parallels, from a variety of sources, are brought to throw an obscure element into relief. As a method it is not easy to handle and to my mind is sometimes overdone since the amplifications can become a means of embellishing the ego or can be used as a defence against realizing an obvious fact which lies under one's nose. Defensive usage does not, however, invalidate the method, but, because of its less valuable uses, it needs employing by one who can see its inner relevance.

The comparative material, i.e. myths or religious imagery, used in analytical psychology for the purpose of amplification, is different from individual experience inasmuch as it has been worked over by many people; it has either been handed down by word of mouth and edited or has been organized purposely through controversy and the like, so that the individual quality has been rubbed off it and to some extent the original creative experience has gone. It can be compared with statistical statements, or perhaps it is more closely like our psychological hypotheses which represent statements felt to be valid enough and useful enough to have general application. Clearly both these comparisons overlook important differences.

The comparative method is useful to a number of people for penetrating and understanding what is general in human psychlogy, it establishes the objective non-individual contents. But it is more than this; through it we can get behind the conscious elaboration to the central core, the common basis which lies behind the myth, custom, ritual or folk tale and individual experience. It points towards the unconscious content—and this is one which may or may not be capable of adequate expression in words, pictures, or acts. It can point to a content which must stand as incomprehensible—an absolute unconscious.

It is the merit of analytical psychology that it has undertaken an extensive study of this comparative material. It has refrained from premature judgement about its nature. It has made possible, however, tentative formulations concerning, for instance, the place of our social institutions in our cultural economy. Thus religion seems in some respects to have contained not only the emergent cultural impulse but to have taken up a compensatory function in relation to the social and everyday way of life. Christianity is a religion of spiritual love and sacrifice; it compensates the prevalent materialistic outlook with its ego-centred and aggressive trends. The compensation was even clearer in the contrast between the Roman Empire and other-worldly beliefs. One can also point to the Eastern doctrine of illusion (*maya*) in a world in which human life was constantly threatened by plagues and floods. I cannot resist the temptation of pointing out here that the function of medical psychology is strikingly similar, inasmuch as our real work is concerned to bring into some measure of conformity with everyday life those psychic elements which cannot find appropriate expression.

The work of analytical psychologists has shown that the great bulk of the mythological parallels have to be drawn from religion because it is here that the objective psyche still lives unconsciously. I need not elaborate this point. Enough papers about it have been read before this Society to assume this, whilst Jung[10] in Switzerland and the late Dr. H. G. Baynes[11] and others have published large volumes on the topic.

[10] *Symbols of Transformation* (Collected Works, Vol. V). London and New York, 1956. *Psychology and Alchemy* (Collected Works, Vol. XII). London and New York, 1953.

[11] *The Mythology of the Soul.* London, 1940.

It is interesting that most of them come from the less-known religious phenomena, from Gnosticism, from early Christianity, from alchemy or oriental sources. The conclusion can be drawn that our society, and in particular its religious organizations, has succeeded in integrating certain contents of the psyche into its structure, but other parts have been left out and still live unconsciously within the human organism, to come to life again under suitable circumstances. All these unassimilated contents were in the past invariably regarded as objective—the images were treated as objective and real. It is as if the collective form had been specially designed to contain those psychic contents which human beings were unable to assimilate, and to hold them at a distance so that the more arbitrary even random activity of their lives could not be realized as part of themselves and they could be left to integrate the more manageable aspects.

By treating religion empirically and by relating it to the phenomena of the psyche an important step has been achieved without indulging in speculation. We need not assert either the absolute reality of religious content or that religion is a flight from intolerable reality (religion is not one thing, but many, and we as psychologists are in no position to make easy assertions about its manifold contents). The two assertions are really statements about reality, a topic already difficult and becoming increasingly so. The belief that certain religions deal with an absolute reality—God—is neither more nor less sensible than the flight theory, though the assumptions lead to different experiences and conceptions of reality. Acting on the assumption, even the experience, of the absolute reality of God leads to one class of development, for instance, mysticism; acting on the belief that it is defence leads in a different direction, for instance, to psycho-analysis as we used to know it. Whichever notion is preferred, we can say that the evidence of religion goes to support the idea of the objective psyche. This leads to further understanding, because there is a parallel between the observation that active imagination is no general method but occurs only in some cases, and the fact that religious revelation has come only to relatively few, whilst the mass of persons maintain their relation to religious experience through the ritual, that is, indirectly. In a similar way direct relation to the primordial images is usually not too common, especially if we take the psycho-therapeutic field as

41

a whole; though we can infer the archetypes, the main bulk of psychotherapeutic work is directed to the foreground of the psyche.

Let us now turn nearer home to view our own house, for I think we can still see the need for myth and ritual here. Our schools of psychology have characteristics analogous to ritual observance, and our societies are not so different from the old cults which centred round a divine truth. We may well say that our truths are not animistic, they are real or scientific truths, but though not identical, they are analogous, and we do better to recognize that in this realm we are the victims of our natures, of the selves which are at once ourselves yet emphatically not ourselves. We cannot free ourselves from custom and rite, we still need our initiations, even stereotyped methods of expression, so that we assume that when we use such terms as projection, identification, infantilism, reality, conscious, unconscious, mind, or psyche, we understand each other. We are, indeed, just as much in difficulty as the most primitive man, but whereas for him it is spirits that are the dangers, these spirits have now become fundamental postulates which grip us and will not let us go. Any development in psychology is resisted, any change in the structure of our hard-won concepts is most difficult to bring about—analysed people have not yet learnt how to manage themselves much better than their predecessors, not even by the most rigorous ventilation of the unconscious psyche, not even by classing their experiences as infantile and living them through, nor by contrasting them with maturity or calling them pathological, not even by the most skilful use of interpretation.

But what is the alternative to this lamentable inferiority, eclecticism, that claim to be enlightened, to take what is best out of every great achievement and to resist the follies, extravagances, and errors that go with it? It is at least a position, but it is too much the spectator's role, the role of one who cannot value aggression as a prime mover in creative work, and there is too much of the cry of 'Let's all agree where we can and have peace.' Lack of conflict is undesirable. Jung said on one occasion: ' . . . peace is unthinkable. Moreover, peace is uncanny because it breeds war.'[12]

[12] *Essays on Contemporary Events*. London, 1947, p. xvii.

So in psychology we do not need to diminish conflict. Indeed, at times I feel disturbed by the alarming tendency to agreement which sometimes makes itself felt, for I do not believe that as individuals we are sufficiently mature, and we need our contemptible, wrong, mistaken adversaries to keep us healthy.

But if we are to eschew eclecticism, and if yet these societies and organizations are to be regarded as containers and reminders of our inferiority, what alternative is there?

It turns on the problem of assimilating units of the objective psyche—the archetypes; that much is clear. It is a procedure which has never been followed before in history because they, the archetypal images, were not grasped as psychological functions. We still do not know whether the correct method is psychological, but that method at least offers the most promising means of doing this.

It was perhaps the realization of this that made Freud view religion historically. In a sense I find myself in agreement with him, though I cannot agree that the intellect is capable of replacing religion, because in religion we can see the image of unity appearing over and over again—the unifying or uniting symbol of the self.

In order to realize the religious content we have to devise a way of treating the psyche as an object just as much as religion treated its god as objective, without, however, letting it get loose from the person. At the same time the conscious culture pattern which constitutes the realm of the ego must not be overthrown, as seems possible.

As far as I can see, the culture pattern which makes the whole procedure at all possible is science, but many phenomena of the objective psyche are the very things which scientists are apt to treat as anathema. They are simply rejected as 'animism'—fearing that the door is opened to revealed truth, and to all that the physical sciences have sought to root out. The scientist, however, is bound to recognize facts, and nobody has ever succeeded in stopping the unconscious from expressing itself in images. Indeed, Jung regards the capacity to form primordial images as innate, and the researches of psycho-analysts on very small children point in the same direction. It is, I think, a fact that the aspect of the psyche that we call the unconscious can only express itself to the conscious mind animistically in primordial images.

43

If this can be shown to be wrong, then my appeal to the scientific conscience falls to the ground.

This is the argument which once appealed to me and still does, but in the interim, certain changes have taken place, for once the assimilation of the primordial images begins, the intellect is caught and undermined, embroiled in an inevitable life and death struggle for existence. The whole procedure becomes most 'un-scientific'; it becomes highly dramatic, chaotic, and arbitrary, and even people with very well-developed minds can, if they overcome their timidity, become seriously disorientated, so that insight seems a weak, useless instrument.

The gradual development which occurs under these circumstances has been described as individuation. Through this process, laying emphasis upon individual rather than collective or social norms, we arrive in the end at the self.

Just as one starts from the totality as an experience in childhood, so one returns to it in later life, though in a different way, and fully equipped with an organized set of thoughts, feelings, sensations, perceptions, standards built out of experiences spreading over the whole of a lifetime.

It is still interesting to observe, even though it be a common, indeed everyday, experience for most of us, how childhood re-emerges in adult people. The infantile contents of the psyche have only disappeared, they have not been left behind for good, and they re-emerge with a kind of significance which points to the self. It is as if the image of the whole had always been there, essentially related to the child—the image of the divine child, the indissoluble unit of wholeness.

Much of the fascination of the psychology of childhood springs from this archetype. One almost feels sometimes as if all the conflicts of the world were to be solved by the child. The idea is to be found particularly in education, and modern education especially, so that this is directed towards creating a child who will create a new world. It is to be found likewise amongst child psychotherapists and also among analysts. It is supposed that preventive psychiatry is almost identical with child psychiatry, as if there were no parents, or, if there were, it were their business to sacrifice themselves for the child. Is this good for the children in the long run? I hardly think so.

The world is not changed by children, it is changed by adults—

that fact is still often overlooked; moreover, it is changed by adults who are able not only to cope with ordinary everyday life but with a bit more, who, in short, have that bit more which will make a contribution of a positive character to society. The developmental growing phase of our life is childhood; perhaps that is why the real self is so often to be found through the past.

Some recent publications from psycho-analytic sources impress me as almost arriving at the self through the study of children. In order to show what I mean let us start from a passage in Mrs. Klein's paper: 'A Contribution to Psychogenesis of Manic-depressive States.' She is discussing the situation which arises owing to the loss of the loved object and the difficulty of assimilating it. She says:[13]

. . . the inside (of the ego) is felt to be a dangerous and poisonous place in which the loved object would perish. Here we see one of the situations fundamental for 'the loss of the loved object'; the situation, namely, when the ego becomes fully identified with its good internalized objects, and at the same time becomes aware of its own incapacity to protect and preserve them against the internalized persecuting objects and the id. This anxiety is psychologically justified.

This paragraph strikes me as confusing because it is compressed within too narrow a framework, because the ego is somehow swollen up and a thing inside itself.

There is difficulty in picturing the process because the ego is 'a dangerous and poisonous' place where no object can be put. Yet we learn that the objects are there: the internalized persecuting objects. Then we hear that the ego is fully identified with its 'good internalized objects' and tries to protect them against the 'internalized persecuting' ones. *What is containing what?* The ego seems to be containing the objects which are persecuting it from without. Either the ego has two functions and is divided into two parts, or else another concept is needed.

If we introduce another term to express the whole with an inside and an outside the formulation can be clarified in import-ant respects; we need to alter the paragraph by substituting the word 'self' for the ego in one context. Then we get the following propositions. The self is a dangerous, poisonous place; there are good and bad objects within the self; the ego, identified with the

[13] *Contributions to Psycho-Analysis.* London, 1948, p. 285.

good objects, fears that it cannot defend them successfully against the bad persecuting ones.

I admit the difficulties of describing this psychic situation in childhood, and have myself pointed out that the ego and the self can become indistinguishable.[14] This is, however, a special situation which does not justify their being identified. I also admit the difficulty of handling the problem verbally in this way, but I think I am justified, because I have struggled with the same problem myself. What I wish to put forward is this: the self or the image of the whole is as much an object as the good and bad objects or the id.

I do not know whether Scott had a similar difficulty in mind when he put forward his intriguing formulations on the 'body scheme', which is defined as embracing the conscious and the unconscious in a condition of integration as follows:[15]

· The body scheme refers to that conscious or unconscious integrate of sensations, perceptions, conceptions, affects, memories and images of the body from its surface to its depths and from its surface to the limits of space and time. In other words, part of the B.S. is a continually changing world scheme—the extended limits of which have to deal with what can only be called the limits of space and time.

This formulation corresponds reasonably closely to Jung's formulation of the self. Scott's notion, however, seems rather to express the circumference with an internal organization, but I can find no reference to a 'centre' in the way Jung sees it, and Jungians naturally want to know why. Nevertheless it has the kind of flexibility which is like Jung's; it extends from cosmological dimensions to the minutiae of embryology. It is a kind of 'subtle body', 'smaller than the small yet greater than the great', as the Upanishads describe the self.

Inasmuch as Freud defined the ego as a body ego it strikes me as desirable that Scott should reconsider his position by stating more specifically than he has done the relation between the ego and its boundaries, between the body scheme and its boundaries;

[14] Cf. 'The Origins of the Ego in Childhood' and 'Some Observations on the Self and the Ego in Childhood' in *New Developments in Analytical Psychology*. London, 1957.

[15] 'Some embryological, neurological, psychiatric and psycho-analytic implications of the body scheme', *International Journal of Psycho-Analysis*, Vol. XIX, Part 3, 1948, p. 1.

because there seems to be the same condensation as that in Mrs. Klein's article. There is a similar confusion about the relation of ego and object.

In analytical psychology the self is usually distinguished from the ego and conceived in the relation of object to subject. It was suggested to me that Jung's difference with psycho-analysis on this point was due to a different concept of the ego. I have looked up Jung's pronouncements upon the subject, scattered through his works, and could find no essential difference between him and Freud in this respect. The ego is the part of the whole which, rooted in perception and so in the body and being the centre of the conscious, yet stretches down into the unconscious. The part of the ego which stretches down is called the shadow and corresponds to Freud's unconscious ego. Jung would not, however, call the super-ego by this name—he allocates it to the archetypal matrix of the psyche.

But why am I making such a bother about the objective nature of the psyche and its relation to the whole? It is because the one cannot be realized apart from the other. In many spheres the concept of the whole is to be found, for instance, holism in philosophy, holistic medicine—whilst we are outraged if anyone tries to undermine our cherished assumption of the personality as a whole, though at the same time we study it in fragments.

But concepts of this kind make little difference; it is the same old story of looking for the self somewhere else or cherishing an ideal of unity anywhere but in relation to our own natures—that horror of horrors! The self can be realized only in the individual and will never be grasped by generalities. It grows out of the sustained conflict between subject and object in the sense in which I have defined them, and the individuality is the only thing which holds in the tension. The self is at first latent and emerges only gradually; when it does so it becomes clear that it also is objective, and through this fact can integrate the otherwise seemingly uncontrollable collective objects or archetypes.

The unintegrated objective psyche is highly autonomous—it leads to mass phenomena such as I have referred to at the beginning of this chapter. It leads to phenomena such as those which Bion has described in so-called groups such as the flight or fight reactions; it leads to the demand for leaders, great men, heroes, and gods. It finds enemies more or less indiscriminately; but I need not continue. As far as we know it is only by realizing the individuality that the autonomy can be handled and integrated.

But what can this individual be? We are so accustomed to think of him as opposed to society—an individualist who looks after his own interests or thinks of society as a kind of nuisance. On the contrary, the individual is the integrate representing society, which is the external reflexion of himself. Society was made by man in relation to his environment, and so is the individual, who is therefore much more a social being than one who is 'socialized'. The individual knows his apparent enemy is part of himself as an objective fact.

But this formulation does not indicate that many individuals in the present sense exist. Society, as Ruth Benedict pointed out, is a specialized product; man has dismembered himself in order to create civilization, and so the development of children involves disruption of the unity of his being so that he can build up his ego. This condition is no longer feasible as a final solution. As our world becomes more of a unit man finds it more and more dangerous to find enemies in it. His one-sided development, which in a sense creates an unconscious, is shaken, and it becomes essential for him to take up those neglected inferior and consequently archaic and infantile aspects of his nature which at first horrify him and which he tends to regard as 'a dangerous poisonous place' or as a chaos, and he omits to realize that from here the self can emerge.[16] He cannot safely go back, and he has to re-establish that unity which he once destroyed without losing what he has established through that quasi-purposive disintegration which produced the ego and so consciousness.

We are at the beginning of our studies in this field. The attempt has here been made to define it, and to formulate the psychological ideas which are to me the most significant and which guide my work as an analyst, and whose expression may contribute towards the objectivity of analytical psychology.

---

[16] This notion is not new. The alchemists, amongst many others, knew it when they used the prima materia to produce the philosopher's stone. They almost reached a psychological position on this topic, but they called it philosophy.

IV

INDIVIDUATION AND EGO
DEVELOPMENT

THE CLASSICAL CONCEPT

THE classical concept of individuation has played a most significant part in the history of dynamic psychology in that it provided a basis for a psychology of maturity at a time when psycho-analytic investigation was emphasizing the infantile components of the psyche. As a sophisticated development, the concept opened the way to the analysis of older people and defined a psychology of maturity distinct from that of childhood. For the last four decades analytical psychologists have been virtually alone pioneering in this field, thanks to Jung's outstanding contribution.

Since, as we shall see, the classical conception, to be outlined first, is not the only one to be discussed, we may consider how stable Jung's view of the subject has been. Many of his formulations have been of transitory importance—they are stepping-stones which are used and left behind; others, on the contrary, bear the hallmark of reliable foundations upon which to build, even though he may sometimes go back to rebuild the superstructure in the light of new discoveries. It would not be possible to list all the occasions on which Jung has referred to individuation, but the subject has been one of the most stable of all his theses.

A germ of the concept is to be found in a letter which Jung wrote in 1913 to Dr. Loy, in which he says:[1] 'The discovery of the value of human personality belongs to a riper age.' In *Psychological Types*[2] he discusses and defines the meaning and symbolism of individuation alongside the problem of types, but it

[1] 'On Some Crucial Points in Psychoanalysis', *Collected Papers on Analytical Psychology*. London, 1916, p. 274.
[2] London and New York, 1923.

was first compactly defined when he wrote 'The Relations Between the Ego and the Unconscious'.[3] which is still the best introduction to the subject. Later a discussion of it is to be found in *Psychology and Alchemy*;[4] in *Aion*[5] the symbolism of the self is elaborated at length, and several essays, published between the major works, give specific indications of the development in his thoughts on this subject.

By 1940 he had come to consider the process as established as a natural phenomenon: 'If the process of individuation is an *empirical fact* [my italics], rather than a theory, one must expect the problem to have its history.'[6] In *The Integration of the Personality* he published two case studies, one of which, together with 'The Idea of Redemption in Alchemy', formed the prototype of *Psychology and Alchemy* in which his most important historical study is begun. The establishment of the process as an 'empirical fact' is important because it undercuts the conception of it as an ideal which Jung has occasionally, I believe mistakenly, taken it to be in no uncertain terms.[7] That images of the self appear in idealized form is not to be denied. It is probable, however, that the collapse of the idealized self image is at the root of the depression and tendency to dissociation which Jung describes[8] as characteristic of his patients for whom individuation is a 'therapeutic necessity' and in whom this difficult and sometimes dangerous spiritual development can be observed to occur.[9]

[3] *Two Essays on Analytical Psychology* (Collected Works, Vol. VII). London and New York, 1953.

[4] Collected Works, Vol. XII. London and New York, 1953.

[5] Collected Works, Vol. IX, Part 2. London and New York, 1958.

[6] 'The Meaning of Individuation', *The Integration of the Personality*. New York, 1939; London, 1940, p. 28.

[7] Cf. *Two Essays on Analytical Psychology*, p. 224, where he says: ' . . . individuation is indispensable for certain people, not only as a therapeutic necessity, but as a high ideal, an idea of the best we can do. Nor should I omit to remark that it is at the same time the primitive Christian ideal of the Kingdom of Heaven which "is within you". The idea at the bottom of this ideal is that right action comes from right thinking, and that there is no cure and no improving of the world that does not begin with the individual himself.'   [8] Cf. below, p. 686.

[9] Jacobi, in her book *The Psychology of C. G. Jung* (London, 1942), went so far as to assert that because of its danger the process should occur only in persons undergoing analysis. By contrast, Henderson ('Resolution of the Transference in the Light of C. G. Jung's Psychology', *Report of the International Congress of Psychotherapy*, Zurich, 1954. Basel and New

The empirical grounds for the conception began from clinical studies. Jung found that after the personal unconscious has been investigated, and so the ego defences sufficiently gone into, a change begins to occur. It becomes increasingly realized that the personality is not controllable by the conscious mind, which is only part and not even the centre of an inner psychic reality. At first this fact is only vaguely appreciated by the ego, which yet, slowly, abdicates from its supposedly dominant position; as this happens the transpersonal archetypal forms, laden with affect, come more and more into the field of consciousness as fantasy images; if the ego relates to these adequately a development begins and progresses in a fairly regular way which can be described in terms of a sequence of images. This has been done so often that there is no need to repeat it here; it culminates in the emergence of symbols of the self, around whose centre the process 'circumambulates'.

To consider individuation in terms of an inner sequence of images, as is sometimes done, is, however, to look at only one aspect of the process, and indeed creates quite a false impression, not only because of the richness and diversity of the living fantasy which develops, but also because it takes insufficient account of the ego and appears to exclude individual differences. The subject of the ego will be considered more extensively later. So as to distinguish individuation from individual differences, which have been made the subject of study by psychologists in various ways not necessarily connected with development (for instance, the intelligence tests), and from individualism, Jung says:[10]

Since the individual is not only a single, separate being but, by his very existence, also presupposes a collective relationship, the process of individuation must clearly lead to a more intensive and universal collective solidarity, not a mere *isolation*.

York, 1955), who has attempted the most systematic account of the progress of an analysis so far, lays the greatest stress on the investigation of the parent-child relationship during analysis and states that individuation only begins towards the end of the analytic development, continuing after its termination when active imagination replaced the analytic dialectic. In this account he lays emphasis on the naturalness of the process. How far these differences are due to contrasting analytical procedures it is difficult to say, but the question of technique clearly forces itself upon our attention.

[10] *Psychological Types*, London and New York, 1923, p. 562.

But what happens to the person? The following gives an outline sufficient for present purposes:[11]

. . . individuation is the process of forming and specializing the individual nature; in particular, it is the development of the psychological individual as a differentiated being from the general, collective psychology. Individuation, therefore, is a *process of differentiation*, having for its goal the development of the individual personality.

It will be apparent, from the account given in the last two quotations, that introversion only depicts an aspect of a process which, in reality, involves the whole personality. Therefore the ego must find more place than would seem to be indicated by a phrase like abdicating its central role; indeed it will be contended here and later that the attitude and strength of the ego is crucial. The process of abdication is in any case not easy, it is only attained through long conflict-ridden experiences:

Consciousness and the unconscious do not make a whole when either is suppressed or damaged by the other. If they must contend, let it be a fair fight with equal right on both sides. Both are aspects of life. Let consciousness defend its reason and its self-protective ways, and let the chaotic life of the unconscious be given a fair chance to have its own way, as much of it as we can stand. This means at once open conflict and open collaboration. . . . It is the old play of hammer and anvil: the suffering iron between them will in the end be shaped into an unbreakable whole, the individual. This experience is what is called . . . the process of individuation.[12]

It will be clear that Jung here describes a development in persons with a well-established ego. Indeed he has underlined the importance of it on numerous other occasions where individuation is conceived as an introverted development in mature people in the second half of life and, though examples of the imagery, the meaning of which will be discussed later, have been observed in younger people, it is only after considerable consciousness and experience of life has been achieved that the development can take place.

It might be held that time and libido are not available for intensive introversion in the first half of life when, at least in our society, the main interest is directed to practical considerations,

[11] Ibid., p. 561.
[12] 'The Meaning of Individuation', op. cit., p. 27.

but the more cogent argument is that the whole process is transpersonal and historical.

There is a tendency for older people to become increasingly philosophic and less affected by the problems and anxieties that beset the young. Some of them develop a philosophy of life founded in a well-organized and so differentiated attitude towards the inner and outer worlds. For such a dynamic structure to be differentiated and stable, considerable experience of life is a necessity, otherwise a closed system is liable to develop which cannot assimilate and modify or even dissolve and rebuild itself in the face of new experience.[13] A philosophy of life, in this plastic sense, is a transpersonal manifestation of personality. As such I propose to include it amongst the manifestations of individuation, which as a transpersonal *opus* has not only personal but centuries of historical development behind it; individuation is not to be conceived as primarily the culmination of the individual's personal history, but first and foremost as the culmination of the history of civilization. Because it is so regarded, Jung has studied the history of symbolism at great length: he finds that the self is expressed in Gnosticism and Christianity,[14] but it is his great achievement to have discovered a true precursor of individuation in the strange contents of alchemical texts which had puzzled scholars for centuries and, for that matter, the alchemists themselves.

To recapitulate: individuation is a transpersonal development resulting in growing consciousness of the self; it begins in the second half of life to continue through it. A considerable degree of ego maturity is required for it to begin and, once started, it leads to a development in consciousness and the formation of an individual philosophy of life giving increasing moral autonomy and a sustained transpersonal attitude to the inner and outer worlds based on the symbolic experience of the self.[15]

One of the, to my mind, vital advantages of adhering to this

[13] For an interesting discussion of this topic, cf. Jung, 'Psychotherapy and a Philosophy of Life', *The Practice of Psychotherapy* (Collected Works, Vol. XVI). London and New York, 1954.

[14] Cf. *Aion* (Collected Works, Vol. IX, Part 2). London and New York, 1958.

[15] The procedure termed active imagination, to be discussed later in a separate essay, is widely considered to be the best single indication that individuation is taking place.

classical view of individuation is that it leads to the definition of characteristics which can be subjected to clinical testing.

It is not out of place, in view of what will be discussed later, to comment here on the fact that the *progression* of images has never been observed in childhood and that, though children make philosophical remarks, nothing like a philosophy of life is ever expressed by them. As a concept, individuation is at best of little use when applied to children, because to understand the structure of their psyche a different concept of the relation between ego and the self is required. Application of the wrong one can be and has been one of the major stumbling blocks in the way of the development of the study of child psychology by analytical psychologists.[16]

THE EXTENDED CONCEPT

The above view of the matter represents, with some minor modification, what I conceive to be the main trends in Jung's argument. That the case in *Psychology and Alchemy* is that of a young scientist must consequently be taken as an exception, for in 'The Stages of Life',[17] 'The Development of Personality',[18] and, it may be added, in many of his essays on psychotherapy, he underlines the importance of the varying aims of life in different age groups in a way which only goes to support the present interpretation of his views in terms of age.

At the end of his definition in *Psychological Types*, however, Jung includes the following paragraph (p. 563):

Individuation is practically the same as the development of consciousness out of the original *state of identity* (*v.* Identity). Hence it signifies an extension of the sphere of consciousness, an enriching of the conscious psychological life.

Definition 25 on 'Identity' states (p. 535):

It is a characteristic of the primitive mentality, and is the actual basis of 'participation mystique' which in reality is merely a relic of the original psychological non-differentiation of subject and object—hence

---

[16] Cf. Fordham, Introduction to *The Life of Childhood*. London, 1944; and 'Child Analysis', *New Developments in Analytical Psychology*. London, 1957.

[17] *Modern Man in Search of a Soul*. London and New York, 1933.

[18] *The Development of Personality* (Collected Works, Vol. XVII). London and New York, 1954.

of the primordial unconscious state. It is, therefore, a characteristic of the early infantile mental condition. Finally, it is also a characteristic of the unconscious content in adult civilized man, which, in so far as it has not become a conscious content, remains permanently in the state of identity with objects.

Though Jung has clearly established that individuation can be observed as the enriching of consciousness in the second half of life, yet the combination of these definitions might easily lead the reader to deduce that he believed it began in infancy.

In spite of his sensible insistence on the clear need for children to adapt themselves to the requirements of society, to which everybody agrees even though the often-implied sacrifice of the inner world to this end is to my mind dubious, there are many passages in Jung's works which could give rise to a wider interpretation of individuation; and when we read that it 'leads to a more intensive collective solidarity' this would make it seem as if there were no theoretical difficulties in taking individuation, i.e. realization of the self, as the aim of a whole life. The aim of the first half of life might then be thought of in a new sense as somehow contributing to the ultimate conscious appreciation of psychic totality.

Perry, though he seems recently to have withdrawn from his earlier position, may be taken as an exponent of this view. He treats individuation as an 'instinct', and then:

This drive toward individuation is apparently a spontaneous urge, *not under the leadership of the ego, but of the archetypal movement in the unconscious* [my italics], the non-ego, toward the fulfilment of the specific basic pattern of the individual, striving toward wholeness, totality, and the differentiation of the specific potentialities that are innately destined to form the particular personality in question. The unconscious is the matrix out of which these various qualities arise step by step toward differentiation in consciousness, which they approach first in symbolic guise until the ego learns to understand and incorporate them. In this unconscious matrix, then, the pattern of the wholeness of the personality lies hidden awaiting the hand of experience to stir it into activity; it is not an ego ideal formed by upbringing, but a dynamic urge emanating from the core of one's being, laden with affect and presenting itself to consciousness in terms of the archetypal symbols.[19]

[19] Perry, *The Self in Psychotic Process*. Berkeley and Los Angeles, 1953, p. 45.

It will be noticed that Perry here implies an innate teleological process, starting from the unconscious.

In *Mythology of the Soul*[20] Baynes also links individuation up with instinct psychology,[21] and he has related it to the physical tendency in animals towards completeness,[22] but elsewhere he says,[23] following Jung, that the process employs an introverted symbolism and leads to the surrender of the ego to the self.

The concept of the process as instinctive is also expressed by Esther Harding,[24] who believes it to be 'the instinct of self-preservation on a higher plane.'

CRITICISM OF THE EXTENDED THESIS

If current views of instinct be accepted, the notion that individuation is an instinct is untenable. The loose use of the term instinct,[25] widely current in analytical psychology, makes it impossible, however, to dismiss the idea thus and indeed often makes any criticism decidedly difficult because of the variety of different meanings given to the word.

The formulations, to which reference has been made above, may be compressed into the statement that individuation is an innate teleological tendency or possibility originating in the unconscious. The ego plays a subsidiary part in it by becoming aware of the processes as they emerge and by integrating a number of ill-defined elements into its structure. It is here that there lies the main difference from the classical concept in which the ego is conceived as taking a major part in the whole development.

Baynes's parallel with the tendency of organisms to repair damage or even to replace lost organs must be taken not as a one to one correspondence with individuation, but in the nature of an analogy, and as such it refers to the synthetic function of the self;

[20] London, 1940.
[21] Ibid., p. 488: ' . . . individuation must be recognized as a primary instinct.'
[22] Ibid., p. 63.   [23] Ibid., p. 266.
[24] *Psychic Energy*. New York, 1947.
[25] This usage is, to my mind, no advantage, indeed in cutting across trends in biological thinking it gives an antiquated air to the thinking of analytical psychologists and tends to get their theories dismissed out of hand. Cf. Fordham, 'Biological Theory and the Concept of Archetypes', *New Developments in Analytical Psychology*, London, 1957.

it is at variance with his acceptance of the place which the ego, defined as the centre of consciousness, takes in the whole procedure.

In introducing a teleological view it needs to be remembered that it took biologists a hard struggle to get away from the sterilizing influence of this view in their own sphere. Jung,[26] possibly realizing this, found it necessary to point out in a footnote that his final energic concept did not imply teleology, and he devoted a large part of one essay[27] to denying the existence of anything like a personality in the unconscious, which is implied in the emphasis given to the innate concept of individuation. The extended conception would indeed appear to necessitate a regression to rather old-fashioned teleology. If the end is pre-ordained in the unconscious, or perhaps it should be said in the self, as the idea of entelechy which is sometimes introduced reinforces, it is difficult to see how either of these postulates could be established. The ideas, to have any scientific relevance, would involve such an enormous advance in the knowledge of hereditary elements that the imagination boggles at it; furthermore they would involve disentangling the acquired elements from those which are innate—an extraordinarily difficult proceeding. But more important is the general trend in psychology to finding the type of prediction here implied, i.e. that there is an inherent aim of a definable kind, more and more difficult.[28] Unconscious aims are recognized as an essential feature of instinctive life whose manifestations can be extended in range by various means of which the interaction between the conscious and the instincts in the unconscious is one. When this happens the rigidity of the instinctual aim becomes modified and transformed in ways that diminish rather than increase the predictability of its manifestations. Indeed the range of possible solutions to any particular problem progressively increases. Thus any specific inherited

---

[26] Cf. *Contributions to Analytical Psychology*, London and New York, 1928, p. 1, footnote 3: 'I avoid the expression "teleological" in order to escape the misunderstanding that attaches to the current concept of teleology, that is, the assumption that teleology contains the idea of an anticipated end or goal.'

[27] 'The Meaning of Individuation', op. cit.

[28] It might be claimed that no definable aim is implied, but if there is not, and only a very general and vague idea of it is needed, I cannot see that teleology need be introduced.

pattern which is conceived to unfold is subject to unpredictable modification.

In this connection it is germane to consider the relevance of synchronicity,[29] defined as meaningful coincidence. The phenomena embraced under this heading are intimately related to the archetypes in the unconscious and so indicate the nature of unconscious processes. The attribute of meaning does not carry with it the concept of purpose, which can result, however, from the wrong preconceptions of ego consciousness—hence the tendency to superstitious conclusions! On the contrary a meaningful coincidence is much more like a chance event, even though the idea of synchronicity involves a radical criticism of the ubiquity of the chance-cause pair of opposites. If this scientific conception is criticized, so also is the notion of an unconscious purposive drive to individuation.

A further serious difficulty in accepting the extended thesis is the clinical material instanced to support it. All analytical psychologists who have sought to extend the concept, Baynes and Perry[30] amongst them, rely upon adult case material, much of it pathological. But whether it be relatively normal or highly patho-

[29] Cf. Fordham, 'Reflections on the Archetypes and Synchronicity', *New Developments in Analytical Psychology*, London, 1957, for an introductory statement to Jung's detailed elaboration of the thesis: 'Synchronicity: An Acausal Connecting Principle', *The Interpretation of Nature and the Psyche*, London and New York, 1955.

[30] Baynes and Perry have both made a special study of the psychotic process; they both found that archetypal forms appeared in it. Perry evidently felt himself in a difficult theoretical position, indeed he modified his earlier view as follows, in 'Acute Catatonic Schizophrenia', *Journal of Analytical Psychology*, Vol. II, No. 2, 1957 (p. 137): 'In acute schizophrenia the central and most dynamic issue, I feel, concerns the self-image; this refers to two interrelated systems, the ego's severely damaged view of itself, and the ego's root archetype, the self, which tends to compensate this debasement with an exalted play of fantasy imagery full of its lost potential. Since I use the term self-image regularly in discussing the problem, I wish to avoid confusion of terms and call the former the *personal self-image* and the latter the *central archetype*; this archetype is here conceived as making its appearance at all phases of life and in all kinds of states of integration and disintegration, and thus is not always associated with the conscious experience of selfhood, in the sense of being an achievement requiring long and arduous work of spiritual or psychological development specifically designated by Jung the individuation process.'

logical, it always shows evidence of a developed ego consciousness, a repressed personal unconscious, and all their patients
show considerable ability in expressing complex archetypal
images, analogous to mythology. These organized forms do not
exist at birth, or for several years after it. On the basis of this
material they all agree, following Jung, that in individuation the
ego gives way to the self, which becomes a 'new centre of the personality'. But what of infants and children, who must inevitably
be given some status on the thesis that the process is innate? In
their case the ego develops away from the self, for the wholeness
of the self is dangerous to them for reasons the exact inverse of
those found in adults.[31] Too little recognition is given to modern
researches into the early stages of ego development in infants, in
whom sophisticated imagery cannot in any case be found, and it
is obvious that no infant could ever have painted the pictures so
far published as manifesting the individuation process.[32] This
subject is further bedevilled by the tendency so often found in
the writings of analytical psychologists about infancy to fit in
with crude and often superseded theories. One of them is that
the child (meaning infant) is indubitably part of the mother's
psyche from birth onwards. This idea, which played a useful part
in the history of child psychology, overlooks that the infant
separates from his mother at birth and has then to go through a
long process of getting to know her as she has to get to know him.
In this process identification takes an essential part.[33]

The extended thesis has, however, some justification in that it
attempts to account for the empirical fact that archetypal images,
including those referring to the self, can be observed in a more
simple form in children and young adults. These facts need to be
met and have led to modification of the classical concept of individuation; the facts are agreed, their interpretation is questionable, and an alternative is to conceive of the images as integrative
elements superordinate to the ego. They may operate in part
consciously or can be completely unconscious, sometimes sup-

[31] Cf. Fordham, 'The Origins of the Ego in Childhood', *New Developments in Analytical Psychology*. London, 1957.

[32] Cf. 'Concerning Mandala Symbolism', *Archetypes and the Collective Unconscious* (Collected Works, Vol. IX, Part 1). London and New
York, 1959.

[33] Cf. Fordham, 'The Origins of the Ego in Childhood', op. cit.

porting, but also threatening, the integrative power of ego consciousness.

Without doubt the observations complicate the theoretical problem, but they do not undermine the classical conception so long as we adhere to the crucial importance of the ego and keep clearly in mind that the study of non-ego integrative processes does not necessarily indicate individuation, and indeed can indicate the reverse.

To solve the theoretical problem set by the discovery of archetypal images, including the self, in all stages of life, it is necessary to discuss early ego development.

EGO DEVELOPMENT IN CHILDHOOD

In a previous paper[34] I quoted Jung in support of a theory that the self is the prototype of the ego; this, together with other considerations, led to the postulate of an original self, which differs from all other states of integration in that it has no subjective manifestations but can be inferred or intuited by observation. The theory postulated an original self which cannot give rise to the ego without dividing up spontaneously into deintegrates; these, by forming the basis for images of the archetypes, make possible the gradual developments of the infant's relation to his mother and himself, and the gradual establishment of the ego over against the archetypal energies. These can at first often be observed to threaten the infant, and would overwhelm him disastrously were he not cared for by his real personal mother who takes responsibility for satisfying his needs and protects him on the one hand from social pressures with which he is manifestly not ready to deal, on the other from the complex inner energies against which he can be equally helpless and against whose effect even the best mothers can sometimes be powerless.

The relation of the ego to the archetypes in infancy is radically different from that in later years; originally the ego grows out of the self, as the result of its spontaneous deintegration followed by its reintegration. This process repeats, so that the self, considered dynamically, integrates and deintegrates in a rhythmic sequence. Gradually ego boundaries form and the psyche gains a demonstrable structure; only then can we refer to the complementary

[34] Cf. 'The Origins of the Ego in Childhood', op. cit.

opposites, the ego and the archetypes, which can express themselves in images. It is recognized that, once this has happened, the energy in the archetypal forms bears a compensating relation to the strength of the ego as the centre of the conscious mind, and so, as the relative dominance of the ego comes about, the archetypal forms sink into the background or get hidden behind the barriers of repression. But when, as happens later in life, the ego ceases to have the same significance, as Jung has convincingly shown, it becomes drained of part of its energy and archetypal activity increases until finally the ego is displaced. It follows that the individuation process begins when ego consciousness, as an ideal and as a social and personal necessity, collapses.

The essential problem lies in the relation of the ego to the self; in early ego development the self gives rise to the ego, which then takes up its own struggle to extend consciousness with the support of, or in opposition to, the self. In individuation the self starts by performing the opposite function; it so to say attacks and eliminates the ego's position of pre-eminence which, as an illusion, it never regains.

INDIVIDUATION AS A SPECIAL CASE OF EGO DEVELOPMENT

Jung frequently stresses the importance of distinguishing the ego from the archetypal images, and so from the self, particularly when active imagination is employed. But this sharp distinction is not always relevant and indeed is only desirable under particular conditions which can be defined as follows:

(1) when a philosophical illusion dominates the scene stating that man's psyche is identical with his consciousness, i.e. when the ego is idealized;
(2) when any radical new development is indicated.

This second proposition is a corollary to the thesis that in infancy the archetypal forms are derived from the self through its deintegration; the deintegrates lead to the emergence of ego nuclei which are later drawn together through the integrative action of the self to form an ego centrum. It would seem that the rhythmic processes of integration and deintegration can be seen reflected in different age groups and in myths, and so repeat through life and have general significance. In my original paper[35] analogies to the theory were drawn from Oriental religions and alchemy, both of which contained further material which it would not be in place to discuss here. I would, however, like to refer the reader to Taoism, in which the twin rhythm which I postulated seems to be part of the central formulations of that mystical philosophy.

If any development is initiated in the self, after the ego is established, its own deintegration is the first step. There is a danger here that the ego may be disintegrated catastrophically in the process if its boundaries from the deintegrates, the dynamic archetypal forms, are not distinguished; the disintegration will clearly be the more extensive the larger the ego. If, however, the boundaries of the ego are clearly defined, the opposition conscious-unconscious is set up after the manner which Jung has described, and the ego, in relating to the archetypal forms, is then in a position either to stabilize or to extend and modify its boundaries by incorporating previously unconscious contents.

When Jung[36] states that he had 'observed patients whose dreams pointed to a rich store of fantasy material without . . . their being able to tell me just where the inner pressure lay', he refers, on the present thesis, to the ego's becoming aware of the deintegrating self. Accordingly Jung sets the patient 'the task of elaborating or developing his theme by giving free rein to his fantasy', and this leads to the 'open conflict and open collaboration' defined earlier in this essay. Jung's technique assists the ego consciousness in defining its boundaries and puts it in a position to collaborate with the self in its 'need' to become more conscious via the deintegrates—the archetypal forms.

From these considerations it becomes possible that individuation is a special case of ego development. But this is not usually so stated, probably because it involves a change in the established concept of the ego and its developmental capacity; further, it requires a distinction between the integrative activity of the self and individuation. It would follow that as the integration of unconscious contents, particularly the shadow, proceeds the ego must not only cease once and for all to be only the centre of

[35] 'Some Observations on the Self and the Ego in Childhood', op. cit.
[36] 'The Spirit of Psychology', *Spirit and Nature*, New York, 1954; London, 1955, p. 412.

consciousness, but it must also be as much an unconscious as a conscious function. It would appear, indeed, that the ego necessarily becomes more and more like the self in being a paradoxical entity; the concept of the self as the archetype of the ego, which is seeping into analytical psychology from various sources, is therefore particularly apt. Jung himself appears to arrive at such a conclusion in *Mysterium Coniunctionis*;[37] there he describes the ego in very much the same terms as the self, adding later an explanation of why this is not inconsistent with his earlier position of distinguishing the ego from the self.

If consciousness becomes only an aspect of the ego, but not its totality, it would necessarily be conceived as a surface phenomenon[38] linked up and organized into a greater synthesis; further the ego and so consciousness could not be demarcated off from the unconscious[39] as heretofore. The result is at once an extension and a limitation of consciousness, which can now rely on more ready access to the unconscious aspects of the ego. Further, the sharp distinction between the ego on the one hand and the shadow and anima (or animus) on the other can no longer be maintained, even though the aspects of the totality represented by them remain essentially incapable of assimilation by the ego. All this depends upon realizing the ultimate nature of the self; it can only be experienced as the symbolic image of the indefinable archetypal totality. The whole can never be known because there is no subject to know it, nor any object to perceive it.

HISTORICAL CONSIDERATIONS

Historical evidence can be used by analytical psychologists in two ways: first it can be scrutinized for archetypal manifestations, secondly it can be investigated to understand how consciousness develops. These two ways of using historical material can naturally be combined in varying degrees.

[37] Vol. I, Zurich, 1955, p. 117.

[38] As Freud conceived it.

[39] It would appear on this thesis that the term 'autonomous psyche' first introduced by Baynes in his *Mythology of the Soul* should only be applied to those states in which the ego is dissociated from the archetypal contents of the psyche. Then the archetypes appear as autonomous images, not when states of integration make the ego and the archetypes part of a whole.

In *Aion*[40] Jung studied the manifestations of the self in early Christianity, gnosticism, astrology, and alchemy, in the main with a view to shedding light on its structure and dynamics; he used history chiefly in the first way. In 'Answer to Job'[41] he has laid more emphasis on the historical process as a development of consciousness, using as his starting point the conflict between Job and Yahweh, next considering how this could have led to the birth of Jesus, tracing the consequences through early Christianity, and leading up in modern times to the Assumption of the Virgin. He ends with the assertion that the main contemporary problem is the assimilation of evil into the image of the self, from which it had been removed during the development of Christianity.

If the study of psychology in childhood has led to confirming the value of adherence to the classical conception, the more general view of it would, at first sight, seem useful in considering the problem historically. The study of archetypal forms in history leads to the idea that as man becomes more conscious, at least as Western history seems to portray it, the idea and experience of God becomes progressively less metaphysical and more psychological. A progressive introjection of the archetypal forms occurs, so that what was only metaphysical becomes, in the course of time, increasingly psychic. Thus the need for the concepts of an objective psyche and of the self becomes apparent, and realization of the self becomes a contemporary issue to be manifested in the life of each individual person. The individual seems to become more interesting in his totality as a manifestation of a historical process which gives increasing importance to the self. From this essentially social point of view individuation as a concept can be used in an apparently broader sense than if each individual life is the focus of attention, and it is overlooked that history is based on a collection of records of adult activities alone; children are not considered.

Individuation is conceived as an historical and evolutionary process. Biological research leads to the concept that all evolution within historical times is the consequence of nurture; heredity plays no direct part in it. Therefore if the symbolic realization of

[40] Collected Works, Vol. IX, Part 2. London and New York, 1958.
[41] *Psychology and Religion: West and East* (Collected Works, Vol. XI). London and New York, 1958.

the self in consciousness is the problem of our era, it would seem inevitable that it can only be grasped by mature persons who have acquired sufficient accumulated knowledge. The acquired conscious mind is then used to bring the self symbol into consciousness. The highly dynamic nature of this event depends upon the reaction of the unconscious to what is primarily an ego activity.

The view of individuation as an extension of the ego is the only possible one on evolutionary theory, which could not support the idea of individuation as an innate process, let alone an instinct. Here the question arises how far children participate in or are influenced by this process. If children sense by empathy changes in the outlook of the times, they can only realize new ones when their conscious mind is sufficiently developed and educated. No innovation of general significance has ever been made by a child. Though he can be conscious of symbolic images of the self, he cannot realize their implications; though he may participate in the general trend towards its symbolic realization, he is still dependent upon his parents for giving him the instruments with which to give it an individual form of expression in his life.

The historical view, which we may reiterate is based on records of the activities of adult persons alone, can therefore only support Jung's original thesis from which we began: 'The discovery of the value of human personality belongs to a riper age.'

CONCLUSION

In treating such a complex topic briefly and abstractly, this essay inevitably makes considerable demands on the reader. My justification for keeping it compact is that clarification of concepts is needed in analytical psychology; the thought in them can be followed more easily if it is not interrupted with illustrative material, of which there is in any case sufficient except from children. An abstract theory is justified if it is so formulated that it can be refuted or confirmed, or if it orientates observers amongst the otherwise bewildering mass of material presented to them. An abstract theory or model is thus an instrument to be used; it must not be discarded until its usefulness has been exhausted and a better one presents itself.

The concepts in this paper are mainly conservative inasmuch as they contest the extension of the classical concept of individuation to embrace the first half of life, but particularly infancy. If

individuation be defined as realization of the tendency to wholeness, it cannot cover the predominantly splitting processes of
early infancy and childhood which lead to the opposition ego–
unconscious. In the second half of life there may be deintegration of the self, but the predominating process is a uniting one,
which leads to awareness of the ego as part of a greater whole, the
self. The extended hypothesis leads in a philosophic direction;
it tends to obscurity in formulation, and needs subdividing if
empirical tests of it are to be made. In itself it cannot be tested,
and overlaps with the concept of the essential unity of the living
process already covered by the self concept.

In its application the almost exclusive emphasis on the internal
object which it can imply fosters illusions rather than the appreciation of realities.

The radical part of what has been discussed comes from the
application of researches into the relation between the ego and
self in childhood which have necessitated revision of current concepts about the relation between the two. The criticism sometimes met with, that the views I have put forward come peri-
lously near, or even actually involve, identifying the two, is
beside the point, and is due to superficial reading of what has
been written. The thesis is continued in the following essay on
active imagination.[42]

[42] Some of its practical applications are considered in an earlier discussion; cf. Fordham, 'Notes on the Transference', *New Developments in
Analytical Psychology*. London, 1957.

V

PROBLEMS OF ACTIVE
IMAGINATION

IN his earliest publication[1] Jung recorded the imaginative life
of an hysterical medium who passively experienced phenomena from the other or spirit world. The case shows that
Jung's attention was, from the outset, focused on imagination
which he later learnt to estimate so highly, not only for its symbolic content,[2] but also because it helped him to induce a psychic
state in which his patients experiment with their own natures;[3]
then individuation begins—it leads towards moral autonomy of
the individual.

The concept of active imagination may be considered a logical
outcome of the theory of complexes, since they are conceived as
affective components of the unconscious with relatively fixed
boundaries, as the words mother, father, or ego complex indicate. As separate entities they can be seen represented and experienced in dream images and in imagination; through them it
is therefore confirmed that boundaries exist within the psyche
surrounding affective components which can be treated as inner
objects by the ego; they personate, as Jung terms the fact that
they can be treated as people as distinct from personalities.[4]

[1] 'On the Psychology and Pathology of So-called Occult Phenomena'.
Psychiatric Studies (Collected Works, Vol. I). London and New York,
1957.
[2] Cf. particularly 'The Spirit of Psychology', *Spirit and Nature*. New
York, 1954; London, 1955.
[3] 'The Aims of Psychotherapy', *The Practice of Psychotherapy* (Collected Works, Vol. XVI). London and New York, 1954, par. 99.
[4] The disadvantage of the theory of complexes is that it implies
atomization of the psyche and gives insufficient attention to the integrative trends which lead to the dissolution of separate entities into a whole;
it thus gives an account of a condition of the psyche rather than all
possible conditions of it.

That Jung himself used active imagination before applying it in his practice is made apparent in the Preface to *Symbols of Transformation*,[5] where he says (p. xxv):

... I took it upon myself to get to know 'my' myth, and I regarded this as the task of tasks, for—so I told myself—how could I, when treating my patients, make due allowance for the personal factor, for my personal equation, which is so necessary for a knowledge of the other person, if I was unconscious of it? I simply had to know what unconscious or preconscious myth was forming me, from what rhizome I sprang.

Before he started to embark on getting to know his myth he had been married for many years and was the father of several children, he had made a position for himself as a psychiatrist and psycho-analyst, and had spent several years making a special study of mythology, of which *Wandlungen und Symbole der Libido*[6] was the outcome. Only then did he deliberately start letting the unconscious fantasy find spontaneous expression and discover how to handle it on his own, as a pioneering experiment. Jung himself is therefore an example of his thesis of the stages of life: the first half was occupied in extraverted achievement, the second in introverted spiritual experience. What he says of active imagination is thus a combination of his own experience within himself with an account of what he found occurring in his patients. In this he extended his earlier recommendation that before a psychoanalyst practises his skill he should himself be analysed.

A more detailed description of active imagination does not appear until 1916, when Jung wrote a paper that has only recently been published.[7] In it he gives a remarkably clear account, which needs little or no alteration today, of what he means by active imagination.

He considers that the process is to be initiated in cases of what we should now call an endogenous depression, for he says:

The occasion for calling upon such aid [the artificial technique of eliciting fantasies] is generally a depressed state of mind, for which no good cause can be shown,[8]

or a vague depressive mood:

[5] Collected Works, Vol. V. London and New York, 1956.
[6] First published in 1912.
[7] *The Transcendent Function*. Privately printed for the Students Association, C. G. Jung Institute. Zurich, 1957.   [8] Ibid., p. 16.

. . . a general, dull discontent which is difficult to grasp, a feeling of resistance to everything, a sort of boredom or something like disgust of a vague nature, a sort of torture which cannot be defined more closely.[9]

This he underlines in *Two Essays on Analytical Psychology*, where a case of a young intellectual suffering from a depressive condition is described.[10]

He then insists on the importance of maintaining the integrity of the ego because it ' . . . differentiates and builds up into a whole, while the collective psyche levels out and breaks up the whole into its parts.'[11]

Next he describes in more detail what happens. The first step is to develop a technique for making the fantasy objective; to implement this idea he recommends writing it down. Once the fantasies have thus been objectified, he raises the question of what to do about them and remarks that they can be abstracted or treated aesthetically, but he does not value these attitudes very highly; he continues with the following interesting statement:

It is technically very simple to note down the 'other' voice in writing and to answer its statements from the standpoint of the ego. It is exactly as if a dialogue were taking place between two beings with equal rights, each of whom gives the other credit for a valid argument and considers it worth while to modify the conflicting standpoints by means of thorough discussion, and in this way to strike a balance or at least make a compromise.[12]

Later, in 1939, his conception of it is almost identical.[13]

---

[9] Ibid., p. 17.

[10] Collected Works, Vol. VII. London and New York, 1953, pp. 211–217.
The case published in 'A Study of the Process of Individuation', *Integration of the Personality*, New York, 1939; London, 1940, suggests a mild depression, for the patient ' . . . came to a region of inner darkness where the road apparently ended' (p. 33).
In 'The Spirit of Psychology', *Spirit and Nature*, New York, 1954; London, 1955, Jung expresses it differently, for he says: 'I had often observed patients whose dreams pointed to a rich store of fantasy material. Equally, from the patients themselves, I got the impression that they were stuffed full of fantasies' (p. 412). It is of interest to compare Melanie Klein's studies of the relation between early infantile anxieties and symbol formation (Klein, 'The Importance of Symbol Formation in the Development of the Ego', *Contributions to Psycho-Analysis, 1921–1945*. London, 1948.   [11] *The Transcendent Function*, p. 21.

[12] Ibid., p. 22.   [13] Cf. p. 52 above.

But writing and conversation are not the only ways in which active imagination can be developed. Some patients will start painting,[14] and Jung also lists those who model in clay or, more rarely, express their fantasies in bodily movement.

In all this he makes it clear that the procedure he envisages is sophisticated; in it the ego takes an active part: '. . . it is no longer the unconscious which has the prerogative of leadership, but the ego.'[15]

The ego represents a system of integrated components partly personal and partly social. This shows clearly in Hannah's discussion of Hugh of St. Victor's conversations with his soul.[16] She says that Hugh sets out with a ' . . . *very* definite program, the program of the Victories, to disentangle his soul from the world and make her one pointed towards God.' This is part of a process in which he uses all the knowledge and ingenuity at his disposal. Hannah shows that the soul is easily experienced as objective by Hugh, this being supported by current belief in the Middle Ages. She does not, however, comment upon why the nature of the soul should correspond closely to the nature of souls in that period, but concentrates attention on the originality of the soul's dicta, as an indication of their genuineness. She states that conversations with souls were frequent then but contained nothing from the unconscious, then points out the passages in which Hugh's account departed from the convention. The majority were, presumably, patterned by the collective conscious of the period in which the individual was living, and so would not be considered active imagination proper, but rather conventionalized exercises in meditation.

It is impossible to eradicate contents of consciousness from imagination, itself a conscious process, but there is a relevant difference between copying and an original creative product; this Hannah underlines. Most writers on the subject of active imagination attempt to formulate criteria of genuine originality; they stress that the form of the images is individual and spon-

---

[14] Cf. 'A Study of the Process of Individuation', op. cit., and 'Concerning Mandala Symbolism', ibid.

[15] *The Transcendent Function*, p. 21.

[16] 'Hugh de St. Victor's Conversations with his Anima', *Harvest*, London, 1954, p. 27. Published by the Analytical Psychology Club, London, for private circulation.

taneous; they contrast it, like Hannah, with the more stereotyped forms of meditation to be found in Yoga and Christian mysticism. The religious forms, it is claimed, are less spontaneous because they are prescribed by dogmatic theology.

I have quoted the general line of argument in the literature because it is by no means easy to assess religious meditation and contemplation as a whole, but I feel on reasonably sure ground in stating that the aim revealed in active imagination is often different.[17] In reviewing the accounts of active imagination it would appear to me, however, that there creeps into them a tendency to judge by prescribed standards of analysts; further, one cannot fail to be struck by the inadequate consideration given to the rather subtle nature of dogma, and of uncritically accepting the quite patent error that the meditations of mystics always follow what is prescribed. On the other hand, the claim which I personally believe to be correct, that the regular progression of images is a confirmation rather than the result of the concept of individuation, is often presented unconvincingly because the complex and often obscure effects of the transference are not taken sufficiently into account.

Others than Jung have reported similar phenomena as the result of using his techniques: Frances Wickes has done so in her book *The Inner World of Man*,[18] which contains a collection of unusual fantasies and pictures collected over many years of analytic practice. She pays little attention to the possibility that these pictures were related to transference manifestations. Baynes[19] has applied the method of painting pictures to the therapeutic analysis of the two cases studied by him; neither he nor Frances Wickes uses the term active imagination. Recently Esther Harding has studied Bunyan's *Pilgrim's Progress* in relation to the subject.[20] Several smaller essays have appeared; Kirsch[21] studied a woman with a great imaginative capacity, stating that the processes he there described were not to be regarded strictly as active imagination because there was no real

[17] Cf. 'The Dark Night of the Soul', below, pp. 130 ff.
[18] New York and Toronto, 1938.
[19] *Mythology of the Soul*. London, 1940.
[20] *Journey into Self*. London and New York, 1956.
[21] 'Journey to the Moon', *Studien zur Analytischen Psychologie C. G. Jungs*, Vol. I, Zurich, 1955.

'confrontation' between the ego and the archetypal imagery, whilst Barbara Hannah has published two longish papers on the subject, 'Some Remarks on Active Imagination'[22], and 'Hugh de St. Victor's Conversations with his Anima' to which reference has already been made.

Zeublin[23] has recently thrown the cat amongst the pigeons by applying the term to material produced by an adolescent child aged fourteen. Since I had previously published play and picture material containing archetypal images,[24] I reacted to Zeublin's paper by suggesting in a brief note[25] that the term imaginative activity might be used to highlight the difference between the ego strength in children's and adults' products. I wanted to emphasize that active imagination is a sophisticated process and a manifestation of individuation; the comparisons with Yoga techniques, Christian mysticism,[26] amongst which the Exercises of St. Ignatius of Loyola feature, alchemy, the creative imagination of artists,[27] and the part of imagination in the formation of scientific theories[28] support this view: all these activities can be, in the best sense, signs of maturity. It is also in accord with this view of the matter that Jung uses active imagination in relation to techniques which reduce contact between analyst and patient to a minimum, i.e. once-weekly interviews interspersed with longer breaks.[29] The patient, he says, becomes active where before he was passive, he suffers from his dependence upon the analyst which needs to be broken and, when this is done, he finds that the state of infantile dependence is gradually transcended: active

[22] *Spring.* New York, 1953. Published by the Analytical Psychology Club, New York, for private circulation.

[23] 'Die Aktive Imagination in der Kinder-Psychotherapie', *Studien zur Analytischen Psychologie C. G. Jungs,* Vol. I.

[24] *The Life of Childhood.* London, 1944. Cf. also *New Developments in Analytical Psychology.* London, 1957.

[25] 'Active Imagination and Imaginative Activity', *Journal of Analytical Psychology,* Vol. I, Part 2, 1956.

[26] Cf. also below, p. 130.

[27] Cf. Jung, 'Psychology and Literature', *Modern Man in Search of a Soul.* London, 1933.

[28] Cf. Pauli, 'The Influence of Archetypal Ideas on the Scientific Theories of Kepler', in C. G. Jung and W. Pauli, *The Interpretation of Nature and the Psyche.* London and New York, 1955.

[29] I have discussed these techniques elsewhere. 'Notes on the Transference', *New Developments in Analytical Psychology.* London, 1957.

fantasy is the 'beginning of independence, a step towards psychological maturity'.[30] Thus the development can be considered in relation to reducing the transference, as will be seen later. Henderson takes a comparable view when he says that active imagination only occurs after the end of analysis.[31] Both Jung and Henderson would seem to agree by implication that to conduct active imagination requires a capacity to be alone, in a positive and creative sense, without isolation and without retreat from the outer world or absorption in a world of fantasy, or being otherwise cut off from outer relatedness.[32]

It needs to be realized that, in the end, according to Jung, even the inner companionship of the symbolic images is dissolved. At first the patient struggles with paints and paper to portray what is within himself through the inner images which present themselves to him spontaneously, but 'In countless pictures he strives to catch this interior agent, only to discover in the end that it is eternally unknown and alien, the hidden foundation of his psychic life.'[33]

ILLUSTRATIVE EXAMPLE[34]

A man in his late forties was able to use his imagination as follows. He would become aware of a mood which he could not control and then he would start to make up fantasies. At first these are quite easy to control and can be stopped at will, but then he gradually becomes aware that they have a tendency to

[30] 'The Aims of Psychotherapy', *The Practice of Psychotherapy* (Collected Works, Vol. XVI). London and New York, 1954, p. 49. It will be appreciated that there have been many other steps, but this is the beginning of the final one.

[31] 'Resolution of the Transference in the Light of C. G. Jung's Psychology', *Report of the International Congress of Psychotherapy, Zurich*, 1954. Basel and New York, 1955.

[32] Hannah lays considerable stress on the concept that active imagination should not interfere with but rather enrich the demands of everyday life.

[33] 'The Aims of Psychotherapy', op. cit., p. 49.

[34] I have used this example elsewhere in another context. Cf. *New Developments in Analytical Psychology*, London, 1957, pp. 58 f. I do this, not because it would not be possible to produce a different example, but because there is no point in doing so. The criticism that the material is repeated appears senseless to me.

become autonomous, i.e. they begin to get an objective reality, and then he sets up some sort of relationship between his ego and the images which he can influence and which can in turn influence him.

To illustrate his experience we may consider the following fantasy sequence beginning at the stage at which the images become objective.

A large magician was able to reduce the sun and moon to a small enough size to go into the holy mountain, but he could not get them into the maze that lay inside there because his hands were too big. He wanted to get the sun and moon into the centre of the maze because if he did so unlimited energy would be provided. As he was a hermaphrodite, he made out of himself a tiny man who did the trick.

Then the position changed, for the patient

got very much upset because the little man got so above himself at accomplishing a feat which the magician could not, that he nearly went up in flames. The excitement went on for several days.

The patient was by now fascinated,

and 'began to care desperately what happened to the little man. After some time an old man with a long beard appeared; the little man liked him and climbed into his hair to fall asleep.'

After this there was a pause in the fantasy, but the mood had not gone, so the patient took an active part in the fantasy.

'I confronted the old man, who, I found, was very much enjoying a tickling in his beard caused by the activity of the little man. I reprimanded him for insufficient care of his charge. The old man, however, was stuffily contented, and paid no attention, so I took the little man away from him and gave him to the large magician who had big breasts. The little man turned into a baby and nestled down contented. This really was the end!'

This example illustrates the following characteristics:

(1) The man was by himself when the process was in operation, i.e. he arranged it so that no outer demands were made on him.

(2) The early fantasy was initiated by the ego but did not at first catch the mood content adequately; then it gave form to the unconscious and the imagination became objective, taking on independent activity at the same time, i.e. it was as uncontrollable as the moon had been.

74

(3) The objective imagery was then experienced as a drama in which the ego was not involved except as a spectator. But next

(4) the man became anxious and concerned at the point where 'the little man nearly went up in flames'. This was the first stage in which the ego again became active, this time in the objective fantasy.

(5) After a pause during which the patient reflected, he (the ego) became more active and intervened in such a way that the fantasy would come to a satisfactory termination.

(6) The inner activity went on for several days, during which time he was meeting other people, and this was partly defensive. It is evident that he did not go on with the fantasy because of anxiety. But it was the feeling of inner concern ('he began to care'), that made him go off on his own again and finish the fantasy, acting decisively in it.

This example can be termed active imagination because there is activity both by the ego and the objective images controlled by unconscious energies. The point needs underlining: the activity of the ego is an essential part of the definition.

IMAGINATIVE ACTIVITY

We can now turn to the difference between the process so far described and play or fantasy in childhood, which I have called imaginative activity; it is at first sight not very great, as Zeublin noted, at least for adolescent children.[35] There would be no difficulty in finding comparable manifestations to all the characteristics so far described as active imagination. Active imagination and much imaginative activity have, indeed, the following in common: they can both be conducted alone, without leading to isolation, and they can both be creative; in each case the inner world has become highly organized; and the ego can initiate the fantasy and become active in it.

The first obvious difference between the two is that play and fantasy in childhood are the less sophisticated of the two processes. Children's fantasies are more primitive and lack the richness and sophistication of the adult material. The second difference is that children usually need objects (toys), supplied by their parents, though they spend time in private fantasy, as in active

[35] Op. cit. Further examples will be found in Fordham, *The Life of Childhood*. London, 1944.

imagination, for which toys are not needed. It may be remarked in parenthesis that though adults will sometimes enjoy toys as much as if not more than children, they never show the same dependence upon them. Thirdly, as imaginative activity leads sooner or later to uncontrolled instinctive activity, even in introverted children. For instance fantasies about fire will lead to play with fire, sexual excitement, and the making of fire in dangerous places inevitably lead parents to be drawn into the game to exercise control of it. So with numerous other forms of play and fantasy, from time to time control is needed by the child himself because his ego is not strong enough, it is not only needed because of his parents' anxiety.

DEVELOPMENTAL CONSIDERATIONS

This summary review is inadequate because of the variety of psychic states manifested between birth and adolescence. It needs to be supplemented by consideration of some of the different states in which imagination is found between birth and adolescence. In the first place it would seem that, since there is no space or time,[36] there can be no differentiation between subject and object, the first form of imagery apart from the object would therefore be the equivalent of hallucination in the adult since it is more likely than not to be the equivalent of the object. Some confirmation of this concept can be gained through observation of infants who treat objects as if they were dynamic images, and then only later distinguish them during the day; at night the identity continues, for they do not distinguish dreams from reality; only gradually is a dream world recognized and only after several years are fantasies distinguished from acts, and then only for part of the time. As the ego gets more established concepts like play, pretend, imagination, mind, get established as features of the child's life. Earlier experiences, which can and do continue into adult life, are not symbolic in Jung's subtle sense, for there is no symbolic attitude, only images of varying intensity closely related to acts and objects.

This condensed hint of the various and complex processes involved indicates the kind of issue which the topic of imagination raises. The subject of being alone constructively is scarcely

[36] Cf. Piaget, *The Child's Construction of Reality*. London, 1955.

less complex when conceived developmentally. Though the infant shares his most important experiences with his mother, he spends much time alone in his cot or pram, etc.; when he is not sleeping his time is spent in complicated preoccupations, of which part is play. As he grows and sleeps less he plays more, only later sharing his play with others whether they be his parents or other children. Play on his own becomes less at two to three years, though happy play alone continues and develops into an inner world of fantasy, private thoughts and dreams.[37]

Some factors in development can be isolated which lie behind the later capacity to be alone creatively: first and foremost we may list sufficient good experiences of the infant's being physically and psychically together with his parents. Thus imaginative activity would seem to presuppose:[38]

(1) Memories of having been whole and united through experiences of the self in infancy and onwards; these occur in instinctively satisfied states, i.e., when instinctual impulses and fantasies are inactive.[39]

(2) Sufficient memories of good instinctual experiences

(a) in feeding at the breast, then feeding with mother in other ways and finally feeding with other loved persons;

(b) in masturbation and the fantasies accompanying it, for it is here that the child begins to take control over his sexual and aggressive impulses.

(3) The following early experiences of being alone must have proved satisfactory:

(a) in the presence of a second person (mother or father);

(b) in the presence of two others (mother and father).

[37] This phase is sometimes called autoerotic, a term which seems to have been adopted from psycho-analysis, by analytical psychologists. It is a curious intrusion, for it is only so called because of the sexual theory of the libido rejected by Jung. In my view the infant's behaviour is better considered in terms of object relations; cf. Fairbairn, 'Object-Relationships and Dynamic Structure', *Psycho-Analytic Studies of the Personality*. London, 1952.

[38] In making this list of the preconditions for being alone, by which is meant a feeling of rather than an actual physical being alone, I have been considerably indebted to the researches of psycho-analysts, and particularly Melanie Klein and D. W. Winnicott.

[39] Cf. Fordham, 'Origins of the Ego in Childhood', *New Developments in Analytical Psychology*. London, 1957.

The most crucial experience here is the primal scene which may be defined as the conjunction experienced by the child in projection on to his parents. It is brought into consciousness by any excited relation between parents which reaches such intensity that the child is excluded in the affective union between the parents. It is an experience which is repeated in the course of development, but only sometimes corresponds to the witnessing of sexual intercourse between parents.

(4) A preponderance of good over bad objects must be symbolized in the inner world before children can enter into it and enjoy play in it.

This list will make it clear that the capacity to enjoy imaginative activity alone rests on the basis of a satisfactory early instinctual life. We may consider it as beginning when children start to play, and from then on becoming more and more stable and elaborate. It contains the ground plan of active imagination, from which it differs in the ways already mentioned; they indicate less ego content. Consequently the fantasies, in imaginative activity, are not deliberately held in consciousness and not approached with the same deliberate aim in view as we find in active imagination.

TRANSFERENCE AND ACTIVE IMAGINATION

Keeping in view the complex developmental processes through which the infant passes before he can construct an inner world and having in mind that this early period is increasingly conceived as the seeding ground of psychopathology, it is not surprising that active imagination, as an aspect of the individuation process, is not common amongst patients who come to analysts for treatment of a distress in which they have become isolated. They cannot stand being alone, that is a main reason for coming to an analyst.

In any analysis there is plenty of imaginative activity, but this, in contrast to active imagination, can seldom be treated as if it had nothing to do with the transference: imaginative activity is usually related to what the patient thinks is required of him or is somewhere an attempt to interest, fascinate, or otherwise manipulate the analyst's affects. This can apply to painting pictures, holding conversations with imaginary persons, clay modelling, wood carving, or to recounting fantasies containing archetypal imagery. All this material may need taking as transference material, otherwise its essential meaning can be lost and the patient is left disorientated in his fantasies.

From the preceding discussion it will be evident that the criteria of active imagination need clear definition, if only because there may be difficulty in separating it from imaginative activity. But this is not all, for no study seems to have been made distinguishing such processed psychotic splitting from hallucination and delusion formation, hysterical dramatizations, or even obsessional reverie. This gap in the literature can only be noted here.

Regarded as part of individuation, active imagination must be considered a process which leads to an extension of the ego through grasping the meaning of the self. It is indeed regarded by some analysts as the best criterion of whether individuation is being undertaken. Barbara Hannah[40] even takes it to be an aim against which the patients develop resistances. The idea here put forward is that the capacity to conduct active imagination is an indication that early development has been good enough for the individual to find enough enjoyment and meaning in being alone in his inner world, and further that he has developed far enough to do this without needing his parents in periods of internal crisis. It may be added that the imaginative process is derived from the archetypal forms which are essentially unconscious and so are not part of the repressed unconscious. It seems to me therefore mistaken to talk of resistances against it, since in mature enough individuals this activity or *opus* brings its own reward. With reference to the analytic processes, it is the consequence of successful analysis of the transference, which it cannot replace. It grows out of the transference, which provides the best conditions for living through developmental deviations and changing them so that the capacity for symbol formation, if absent or defective, can be increased. The progression in the transference from dependence to independence, from immaturity to maturity, may be conceived as corresponding to the change from imaginative activity to active imagination; the study of transference may therefore be expected to make possible the

[40] *Spring*, 1953, op. cit. She spoils her thesis to my mind by taking an almost moral line about it.

clearer distinction between the two forms of imagination which is needed. It is impossible to say that there is no transference in any particular patient; indeed it may be that so long as a person is a patient we should refer to active imagination only in a qualified sense. This corresponds to Henderson's view.[41] He states that active imagination is a form of self-analysis; but ' . . . the trouble with self-analysis,' as Main[42] has wittily pointed out, 'lies in the counter transference'. Thus, though it is easy to define active imagination roughly, attempts at its more precise definition lead to problems which in the present state of our knowledge cannot be solved.

In conclusion I feel it necessary, because of the prestige which active imagination has tended to acquire, to state that I cannot agree with those who hold that individuation can only occur when active imagination takes place. Active imagination is a valuable indication of its occurrence, because a creative and individual process is seen in operation and an extension of the ego through realization of its relative status within the psychic whole will be the outcome, but individuation can take place without any such elaborate procedure. It must surely occur in anybody who lives a full and rewarding life.

[41] Op. cit.
[42] 'The Ailment', *British Journal of Medical Psychology*, Vol. XXX, Part 3, 1957, p. 130.

VI

JUNG'S CONTRIBUTION TO SOCIAL PSYCHIATRY[1]

IT is one of the surprising features of analytical psychology that little has been published on the subject of social psychiatry, although its whole theory and practice is permeated with social (collective) meaning. Only Ira Progoff's book, *Jung's Psychology and its Social Meaning*,[2] and two researches, one by Plaut entitled 'Research into Transference Phenomena'[3] (in which he tested a hypothesis that groups could be used as a research unit), and another by Lewis[4] (on children's groups in the so-called latency period), supplement Jung's own researches. Ira Progoff's useful volume is almost entirely expository, and Plaut's and Lewis's researches, though highly interesting, do not modify Jung's thesis. It is the aim of this article to discuss Jung's approach, though not to give anything like a complete exposition.

It is forty years since Jung started to formulate his ideas on the collective unconscious. This concept inevitably suggests that of a group mind, a sort of general entity in which persons are immersed—an unconscious of vast dimensions, often believed to have quasi-mystical characteristics. Apart from this fanciful concept it is very tempting to postulate a group mind because of the phenomena of mass psychology and the tendency of groups to behave in typical ways. This tendency has often been recorded, and recently it has been studied in small, leaderless and socially

[1] A paper read to the staff of the Marlborough Day Hospital and published in *The International Journal of Social Psychiatry*, Vol. I, No. 1, 1955.

[2] New York, 1953.

[3] *Report of the International Congress of Psychotherapy, Zurich, 1954.* Basle and New York, 1955.

[4] 'The Functioning of Group Play during Middle Childhood in Developing the Ego Complex', *British Journal of Medical Psychology*, Vol. XXVII, Parts 1 and 2, 1954.

orientated groups. To Jung, however, this typical behaviour is due not to a group mind but to the archetypes of the unconscious whose roots lie in each man; therefore according to him the 'psycho-pathology of the masses is rooted in the psychology of the individual.'[5]

Alongside the concept of archetypes runs that of the conscious mind, which may almost be regarded as a separate entity, having a nucleus—the ego—which is able to organize the field of consciousness into a flexible structure, a structure in which either the perceptive functions, sensation and intuition, or the rational functions, thinking and feeling, predominate or contribute. The ego regularly reacts and organizes the contents of consciousness into an attitude which is defended against all attacks with considerable vigour. The ego can take up an attitude facing the outer world, i.e. it can be extraverted, or facing the inner world, i.e. it can be introverted. Sometimes it does one, sometimes the other, but in most persons it usually does more of one than the other. In contrast to the collective or transpersonal unconscious, which is objective, conservative, and as far as we know unchangeable, the conscious is individual, flexible, and varies greatly in its extent and content.

The ego is conceived as originating from the unconscious after the manner of a child that is conceived in and born out of its mother. But once it becomes established a more or less uneasy and compensatory relation is established between the two. Under conditions of mental health, this relation may be profitably compared to the homeostatic systems of the body,[6] but it differs from these systems in being progressive. The cultural forms of civilization result from the interaction of the conscious and the unconscious.

The exquisitely dynamic relation between the conscious and the unconscious is an essential feature of Jung's concepts. Failure to grasp this point leads to much confusion, for it is impossible to understand an essentially dynamic relation in terms of static concepts. By way of illustration it may be pointed out that though Jung holds it to be true that the 'psychopathology of the

[5] 'Individual and Mass Psychology', *Essays on Contemporary Events*. London, 1947, p. ix.
[6] Cf. Storr, 'A Note on Cybernetics and Analytical Psychology', *Journal of Analytical Psychology*, Vol. I, No. 1, 1955, pp. 93 f.

masses is rooted in the *psychology of the individual*' and not in a mass psyche, yet he would probably recognize that for certain conditions of consciousness, such as that of a social scientist, who considers human beings in the aggregate, a group concept is inevitable. On the other hand, if the problem of developing individual consciousness is emphasized (as it is in analytical psychology) the concept of a group mind becomes an 'as if', and the source of the group activity becomes located in the individual. It will be apparent that this makes psychological truth relative inasmuch as what is true for one condition of consciousness is untrue for another.

In his book, Progoff gives a good deal of space to the subject of symbols and their role in civilization. As we have seen, Jung's analysis is unique, particularly suggestive and difficult to grasp. Therefore, though it has been discussed earlier, the conclusions may be briefly reviewed here. The archetypes express themselves in images, and only through these can the ego become aware of their activity. But the images do not become symbols until a relatively specific attitude of consciousness is taken towards them. This attitude is complex, but its essential core is as follows: the images are not only observed but are made the object of reflection and given value. This attitude is commonly found in religion; it is commonly absent in psychiatric and psycho-analytic literature, where the images are regarded as metaboles, i.e. indications of more significant memories or more disagreeable or horrific experiences. The symbolic attitude is therefore one amongst others, but all of them presuppose an established conscious mind.

This consideration makes it clear (and Jung and his followers bring forward cogent evidence in support) that the mere occurrence of myth-like images does not necessarily involve their becoming symbols. It must, however, be admitted that the images are often confusingly so called in the literature, but if the two usages of the word be kept in mind it will be clear that many people who dream or fantasy in mythical forms are not regarding the images as symbols. It is soon possible to tell if they are not being so regarded, for then nothing seems to happen except that the unconscious dreamingly reiterates its eternal images as if for itself. It is only when the suitable conscious attitude is brought into relation with the images that they become symbolic and consequently creative and transforming.

If the images, which of necessity arise spontaneously, be regarded as symbols, a new consciousness is created. This is recognized by Professor Toynbee,[7] when he says that religious motifs take an essential part in the development of a civilization, for he implies that the symbolical attitude is the creative one as far as history reveals. This accords with Jung's view of the matter, according to which the unconscious is regarded as the mother of consciousness; but Toynbee takes history whereas Jung takes the psyche as his frame of reference.[8] The symbolical contents of Christianity, or for that matter of any other religion, can therefore be valued positively. The insistence upon the historical and physical truth of the Virgin Birth and the other miraculous episodes in the life of Jesus, and of His real Resurrection, cannot be brushed aside by any of the familiar means, for they are truths for a particular state of consciousness. The insistence that they occurred in the flesh is important, even essential, for without this the concrete and objective character of archetypal images could not be appreciated till the psyche so to say appeared as the source of them. Only because they were so regarded at the time could they have produced the radical consequences whose results we witness around us every day of our lives. The attitudes of consciousness which made these non-rational 'truths' real were, and still are, relatively valid from a psychological position.

The historical stages in the development of consciousness have interested many analytical psychologists, as Erich Neumann's volume *The Origins and History of Consciousness*[9] testifies. In this research he deals with the role of archetypes and their symbols in considerable detail. It is a comparative study embracing the myths of the world and he gives highly significant interpretations of them. In particular, Neumann attempts to set out to show in detail the stages of consciousness to which the symbolical images give rise.

But the beliefs of early Christianity and the concrete symbolical attitude are by no means only historical. The firmness with which it is held even today must have surprised many who

[7] *A Study of History*, London, New York and Toronto, 1933 and 1949.
[8] Cf. 'The Basic Postulates of Analytical Psychology', *Modern Man in Search of a Soul*. London, 1933, pp. 200 ff.
[9] London and New York, 1954.

followed the recent controversy over Mrs. Knight's broadcast, 'Morals without Religion', from the British Broadcasting Corporation.[10] Nevertheless, for many it is difficult to allow the concrete attitude any validity at all, except as a phenomenon of extraordinary persistence. To them the real dynamic of civilization springs from scientific discovery in general and the horrid spectre of half the world devastated by atom and hydrogen bombs in particular. 'Behold now Behemoth which I made . . .' But this time it is not God but man who has done the making. For those who grasp this state of affairs, and who realize the non-rational nature of religion, the 'truths' of Christianity need not be proved or disproved; they need reinterpreting so that the symbolical attitude is not submerged and lost to view.

Today the concrete symbols seem to be those of science and the often unrecognized mythology that surrounds it and informs it with life. In spite of this the past and the present are not fundamentally discontinuous, though the expression of archetypes may be so different that the continuity seems to get lost.

It is one of Jung's achievements to have developed a comparative method whereby historical facts can be compared with events going on at the present time, not only in the conscious but also in the unconscious. It is common knowledge that using this comparative method Jung has been led into making what is often called a 'diagnosis of our time', and he has gained a certain notoriety by making predictions about social events of importance. He stated in 1918[11]—his most successful prediction—that a violent eruption of the unconscious was highly probable in Germany. It is, of course, possible to quote other authorities who said the same thing, perhaps not quite so early, but still early enough to be impressive. It is not, however, the relative correctness of the prediction which is specially important, but rather that it was made on the basis of a new method derived from the conception that the psychology of the masses is rooted in the

[10] Cf. *The Listener*, Vol. LIII, Nos. 1350 and 1351, January 13 and 20, 1955, and subsequent numbers for the replies. Mrs. Knight addressing herself 'to the ordinary man and woman whose attitude towards religion is that they do not know what they believe', argued that in these circumstances it was mistaken to try to impose a set of beliefs on children which were not those of their parents. In the course of her argument she criticized the beliefs of Christianity for their lack of rational coherence.

[11] Cf. 'Ueber das Unbewusste', *Schweizerland*, June and July, 1918.

individual. This point of departure leads to the conclusion that the individual can be treated as a sample of the group, a view whose practical application has the advantage of being relatively simple. Now supposing it is found that a number of individuals show the same syndrome, then the next step of comparing the syndrome with observable phenomena in society seems worth taking.

Jung was in a particularly good position to employ this sampling technique, living as he does in a country which has consistently and successfully adopted the policy of neutrality, and in circumstances conducive to the maintenance of an attitude of impartiality. His international reputation brought a large variety of people of different nationalities to his consulting room, and thus he was provided with the necessary comparative material. It was from this position that, with the aid of his comparative and historical method, he developed his 'diagnosis of our time' and elaborated his definition of modern man,[12] both of which therefore rest upon the special method he had elaborated, i.e., they cannot be regarded as just intellectual speculations. The following quotation, which was made in relation to Germany, but is also applicable, *mutatis mutandis*, to other nations and groups, will give the gist of his conclusions:[13]

I observed the German revolution, as it were in the test-tube of the individual case, and I was fully aware of the immense danger involved when such people crowd together. But I did not know at that time whether there were enough of such individuals in Germany to make a general explosion inevitable. However, I was able to follow up quite a number of cases and to observe how the upheaval of the dark forces deployed itself in the individual test-tube. I could watch these forces as they broke through the individual's moral and intellectual self-control, and as they flooded his conscious world. There was often terrific suffering and destruction; but when the individual was able to cling to a shred of reason, or to maintain the bonds of human relationships, a new compensation was brought about in the unconscious by the very chaos in the conscious mind, and this compensation could be integrated into consciousness. New symbols then appeared, of a collective nature, this time symbols reflecting the forces of *order*.

[12] Cf. Jung, 'The Spiritual Problem of Modern Man', *Modern Man in Search of a Soul*. London, 1933.

[13] Cf. 'Introduction', *Essays on Contemporary Events*, London, 1947, pp. xi–xii.

The special feature of the German revolution was that the consciousness of people as a whole, or even of an insufficient number of individuals, was totally inadequate to meet the eruption of the unconscious. They were simply swallowed by it, and so the element of relatedness, to which Jung attaches such importance, was lost. The essential problem is conceived as universal, however, and cannot be simply set aside as a phenomenon peculiar to one country. Obvious signs of the phenomena he described are indeed widely apparent.

Jung's conclusions may be summarized as follows: The more each individual in society is conscious (and this means reacting to social phenomena) the less will there be the danger of the sort of thing that happened recently in Germany. This conclusion manifestly gives a special meaning to psychotherapeutic endeavours.

Analysts and psychotherapists always handle individuals either alone or in small groups. It follows that the methods used to bring about changes within the individual cannot be overlooked, for it is an increase in consciousness and capacity for relationship which is vital. It would seem essential that any method which acted unconsciously and without taking the transference relationship seriously into account must be subject to serious critical examination from the viewpoint of social psychiatry. From this it clearly follows that many of the means used by psychiatrists to bring about, whether by psychological or physical means, so-called 'social cures' are really socially dubious because of the failure to consider in any but the most superficial way the relation of the individual to society. Too often no attempt is made to explore carefully the deeper relations between a patient and his fellows, let alone to understand the nature, structure, and deeper needs of society. All therapies that do not take into consideration the important place which the ego defences and ego attitude occupy in the patient's psychic economy need to be reduced to the minimum. In this context the traditional medical criteria are inadequate, for the health or disease of an individual needs to be considered not in relation to a single person but to his environment as well. Many of the therapies to which I am referring are justified on the grounds that they produce greater social adaptation, by which is meant conformity with the particular ways in which society requires people to behave. The underlying mechanistic metaphysic is often only too clear in this superficial assessment.

Even the biological concept of adaptation, from which the concept of social adaptation is derived, is not mechanistic, for it is related to evolution and so involves the inter-relation between the organism and the environment.

Jung has repeatedly insisted that the psyche cannot be handled with mechanistic concepts alone, not only because it is non-rational in important respects, but also because it is creative. If this creative element is not to be left out, it will be readily agreed that the question should be considered whether a particular individual needs to be more or less sociable at any particular time.[14]

By and large, I suppose, we should all agree that most patients are not socially creative. But at the same time their more limited creativeness may, and sometimes does, lie masked behind a neurosis or psychosis and collides with society.

In short, social adaptation needs to be conceived as a process of interaction between the individual and society. When it is conceived quasi-mechanistically, so that society is automatically right and the individual wrong, it is bad for the individual and for society as well. I am reminded here of a group of children in a hostel who formed a spontaneous 'parliament'. They made a law that no stealing was allowed 'except for those who could not help it'! The exception covered the case of one boy who was so delinquent that nobody could do anything about it. The hostel ran perfectly well on this basis, but in the end the child went to an approved school because he stole not only in the hostel but in the larger society where there were too many people with a less developed capacity for moral discrimination than that of the children. In a sense this child was more adapted when he stole, and he needed not to be condemned or reformed, but to grow through it. A society that supports its members in a crude and too limited moral attitude needs changing. From this and other cases it can be concluded that it is just as worth while examining society as it is worth while studying the individual in any par-

[14] Cf. Jung, *Practice of Psychotherapy* (Collected Works, Vol. XVI). London and New York, 1954, p. 70 f.; Sechehaye, *Symbolic Realization*. New York, 1951; D. W. Winnicott, 'Meta-Psychological and Clinical Aspects of Regression with the Psycho-analytic Set-up', *International Journal of Psycho-Analysis*. Vol. XXXVI, Part 1, 1955.

ticular case. Social psychiatry has the possibility of keeping this end constantly in view, just as does social medicine.

The boy was not in any sense a creative personality. Those real creative people are essential for us to preserve, since great advances come from them. They are significant in this context because they illustrate in a very marked way the need for studying society in relation to individual personalities and they make nonsense of the mechanical view of social adaptation.

Psychologists, psychotherapists, and psychiatrists spend much of their time with human beings; their attention is turned inwards to everyday events in relation to their personal historical antecedents, but eventually to the archetypes of the unconscious, which cannot be avoided even if they go by another name—they 'speak' to our patients' conscious just as they did in the past, though if the more primitive beliefs are lacking they appear as psychic or environmental determinants in the lives of individuals.

Social psychology cannot leave the matter simply as an individual issue. It necessarily deals with groups, and the individuals in a group become more and more archaic, more and more archetypal, less conscious, less differentiated, the larger its numbers become; in other words, they become more historical. It therefore needs special techniques and special knowledge to handle the lower level of consciousness. Amongst the various techniques and knowledge required of a social psychiatrist, perhaps the need for him to be an historian of the psyche stands out most. It is just as important as it is for analysts to relate their patients' material to what has gone before and to recognize historical material when it emerges.

It is this point of view that has been productive and is perhaps a significant contribution of analytical psychology to the social sciences.

There is much to be said (as a recent paper by Abenheimer elaborates)[15] for the thesis that analytical psychology does not belong to the natural sciences, but should be classed with the human sciences, to which the historical and, I should like to add, the comparative methods can be applied. Analytical psychology, at least, employs both these methods and in doing so manages to handle those less tangible aspects of human nature which defy

[15] 'Critical Observations on Fairbairn's Theory of Object Relations', *British Journal of Medical Psychology*, Vol. XXVIII, Part I, 1955.

logical and causal explanation but which are essentially irrational and prospective. Social scientists do indeed often recognize this, if only indirectly, in their use of anthropological findings. This is a tacit recognition that the methods employed with and the knowledge gained from the study of savage societies is useful. In confirmation of this view, Ruth Benedict's comparative researches on sexual culture patterns stand as a fruitful consequence of this thesis.

But neither history nor anthropology goes far enough, for integrating concepts are needed to co-ordinate these and the various other relevant disciplines. It is here that Jung's concepts can come into their own. With beautiful simplicity those of the conscious and the unconscious embrace the contradiction of man's eternal sameness on the one hand and his great plasticity on the other; they make it possible to interrelate the individual and the group of which he is a member, and to reach conclusions of far-reaching importance in the spheres of both individual and social psychology.

The concepts whose elaboration only is complex are united with methods which it is not possible to go into here, but which it may be stated are unfortunately not simple at all. But they are not more difficult than those of other disciplines of less central significance.

The methods can be used only by trained analysts, but the concepts have been used by many distinguished men who have found that their work can be illuminated in essential respects by Jung's researches. This fact has been demonstrated by the annual meetings of scholars held at Ascona in Switzerland.[16] In these deliberations Jung for many years took a central position.

---

[16] The lectures appear in the *Eranos Jahrbucher*, published each year by Rhein Verlag, Zurich.

VII

REFLECTIONS ON INDIVIDUAL
AND COLLECTIVE PSYCHOLOGY[1]

T HE problems involved in the crisis through which we are
now passing[2] are so vast that one can only hope, with the
knowledge and understanding we now possess, to adopt an
attitude towards them. Since we ourselves are contained within
the crisis it may well be doubted whether we have sufficient
objectivity to value it correctly, and so any attitude we adopt is
bound to be provisional.

Supposing we were Chinese, we should undoubtedly look at
the crisis in an entirely different way, if only because the Chinese
nation is much older than we, has survived a very large number
of devastating situations, and has developed a different and more
fatalistic attitude towards them. We might well borrow from
them, if we were able, their relative unconcern for human life
and even their capacity to look at world events more from the
point of view of eternity; if this were possible we should cease to
burden ourselves too much with the sensational and terrifying
questions of our own immediate future which undoubtedly press
heavily upon us. The imminence of our present danger makes it
urgent to find somebody who is not affected by the crisis and
who could dispassionately evaluate it for us; but this is next to
impossible, for all the civilized peoples of the world are contained
in it, and therefore we have, like the hero in the belly of the
monster, first to cut ourselves out from within with what weapons
we can hastily improvise. Therefore what we need is an objective

---

[1] Based on a paper of like title given at a meeting of the Medical
Section of the British Psychological Society on 26 March 1947, and
published in the *British Journal of Medical Psychology*, Vol. XXI, Part 2,
1948. It was prompted by Dr. Bion's address from the chair: 'Psychiatry
at a Time of Crisis', Ibid.

[2] Refers to the state of mind dominating the post-war era.

weapon to deal with the situation. To construct this it is necessary to modify the outlook with which medical psychology easily becomes identified and to extend it by going behind its original frame of reference.

In his recent address from the chair Dr. Bion[3] raises problems related to the wider aspects of psychiatry and psychotherapy in an empirical spirit with which I am in fundamental agreement, but he has left out a great deal which appears to me important. I am critical of his failure to pay sufficient attention to what is surely in the forefront of our minds: that our crisis is essentially one of values. This is implied but never openly stated in his paper. Further I regret that he has omitted more than passing reference to the work of Jung, who has repeatedly made vital contributions to the psychological aspects of the crisis in our civilization and has gone far towards creating the objective instrument which we need.[4] Because of these omissions Dr. Bion's paper has tempted me to put forward some reflections based on Jung's work. In offering them I would like none the less to express again my appreciation of the attitude Dr. Bion has taken up even if I think it fails at just the point where I would have liked him to take a different stand.

The work of psychiatrists with psychological leanings has always had value implications which have not been taken up, though the tendency to pay more attention to them has come very much to the fore since the war. It appears to have grown out of psychiatric experiences in the army.

Analytical psychology has from the beginning studied the basic values upon which psychotherapy rests; in doing this it has had to neglect formal psychiatric considerations and start its development by differentiating a collective aspect of the psyche, the collective unconscious, to the study of which the major part of its energies have been directed. The development of interest in collective or group psychology, which has grown up during the war, can therefore be welcomed by analytical psychologists.

[3] Dr. Bion's studies in group phenomena will be well known.

[4] It is worthy of note that Jung's first paper on the subject of the crisis in civilization appeared in 1918 under the title "Über das Unbewusste", *Schweizerland*, Vol. IV, No. 9 and Vol. IV, No. 10, 1918. *Essays on Contemporary Events* (London, 1947) contains Jung's reflections on the problem of Germany and his attitude towards the German phenomena.

Before proceeding to my more detailed argument I think we should be clear on one point: there is a danger that in extending our researches to collective psychology we may lose our interest in the individual. This would be a disastrous proceeding, especially at the present period of organization and planning.

Fortunately the group and the individual are not as separate as they appear, and it did not take long for analysts as a whole, but Jung more than any other, to realize that any radical analysis of the individual forced upon their notice fundamental conceptions and attitudes, emotional or abstract, which form the basis structure of our society. These have to be made conscious and handled if the patient is to resolve the transference situation and so his own problems. According to analytical psychology, the whole personality of the doctor and the patient must come under fundamental review, and the analyst, as well as the subject, changes before he and his patient finally separate. Just as the fundamental attitude of the analyst towards his patient and so his own valuation of him must sooner or later come under review, and just as he must refrain from concealing his attitude, so also must we present our attitude toward and valuation of society. This necessity has been recognized much more by the critics of analysis, by those who have stood outside its development, than by analysts themselves, who have usually been misunderstood in consequence. To a certain extent this is the fault of our profession which has, until recently, had far too little to say about the topic.

If we are going to approach society from a psychological and analytic position we need to define as clearly as possible the spirit[5] in which we do it. This leads us to our professional roots.

Inasmuch as analysts are doctors, they belong to a cult within which they are confined and are more or less invulnerable. By this I mean that when they concern themselves with symptoms, diseases, and their cure, they are sheltered and protected from external interference and criticism and, at the same time, they shelter and protect an essential attitude to life, health, and disease. This attitude can naturally be expanded to apply to groups, small or large, so that many of the classical sins of humanity can be considered in terms of diseases. Psychiatrists do this,

[5] I should perhaps say that the term spirit might well be thought of as the essence of the subject, the hidden attitude which informs us and which cannot be put exactly into a formal statement.

but they should make it clear, at least to themselves, that in doing so they are modifying a very ancient and significant religious principle, the sense of sin and guilt. Those who are seriously concerned with psychotherapy need to grasp that directly they take up a therapeutic attitude the disease process automatically becomes an evil which they want to eradicate and replace by health, which is a good and desirable state of affairs.

The analytical position is, however, different from the medical one, because it applies the scientific spirit more precisely and so must humbly set itself the sole aim of increasing knowledge, i.e. self knowledge. In consequence it could never confine itself to medical considerations alone, but must encroach upon other fields than psychopathology in which it began. As a result it has been forced to grapple with philosophy, religion, education, and the law, and to comment upon them as Dr. Bion himself has done. Earlier[6] I have referred to the position of analytical psychology in relation to mysticism and philosophy, but only to show that it is neither mystical nor philosophical in its nature. Here it may be added that a good deal of work has been done on the relation of psychology to religion, which obviously differ in their frames of reference. Briefly, religion claims to deal with transcendent realities which cannot be reached by psychological means: but the frames of reference are psychological in nature so that reconciliation is difficult. Much philosophy is just as difficult to reconcile with psychology, though on different grounds; since by means of reason the philosopher claims to decide on matters which actually belong to the psychology of emotion.

Religion and philosophy are both group phenomena, and if we are to follow the scientific spirit in our study of groups large or small, it is necessary to collect facts about what is going on in them; but at the same time we need a means of understanding them, we require an attitude from which we can interpret as well as collect. The two processes, interpretation and fact-finding, must go hand in hand and, as we know from analytical experience, facts very often *only come to light as the result of interpretation*. Moreover, facts by themselves are relatively useless; they need a framework in which to be set and through which they can be digested. Unless this is done we get nowhere; it is like having food set before us with no means of taking it into ourselves, let

[6] Cf. 'The Development and Status of Jung's Researches', above.

alone digesting it. It has always seemed to me that the analytical schools, even where they are wrong or limited, possess an advantage over others inasmuch as they have a system for cooking and digesting otherwise raw food, i.e. the facts. I have taken up this point because Dr. Bion in his paper holds that in dynamic psychiatry we have an instrument for fact-finding. I agree, but we also have an instrument for interpreting the facts; this is as important as fact-finding itself.

In an opening paragraph of this paper I took the analogy of the hero within the monster to illustrate our present situation. This analogy is an appropriate one from which to view a section of Dr. Bion's paper, for he hews out of human psychology certain properties: technical skill, emotional states, and intellectual functions. Having made this excision he goes on to state that our emotional development lags far behind our technical skill. Of intellectual and emotional factors, the emotional ones need most attention, since intellectual development, if it is not adequately catered for now in our schools, is likely to become so, as far as is humanly possible. Yet his statement is but a fragment of the problem and it is clearly inadequate as a complete diagnosis. This Dr. Bion must know very well. He evidently extracts what is necessary for his purpose, and I assume that to be his intention, but why does he not include feeling valuation, since the present crisis is concerned with the question of values? Possibly he intended to place them under the heading of emotion, with which I would not agree.

One of the great difficulties of dealing with values is that they have tended to defy scientific treatment. But they are facts, and it would not be scientific to rule them out of account because they do not seem to be easily subjected to the kind of treatment with which natural science is familiar, or because they are difficult in being subjective. The fact that man has always valued his experiences and his knowledge is certainly true; it is a datum, and scientists betray their science if they ignore it. Consequently, if we are going to be scientific, values cannot be left out. In order to include them we have, however, to stop at the point of expressing them and, at the same time, confess that they are subjective. This position makes values relative, but by taking them in this way, they are accessible to investigation. Not only this: by making values relative, a step forward is taken of the most significant kind in the direction of individual moral responsibility.

I have called this paper 'Reflections on Individual and Collective Psychology'. In differentiating between the two I do not mean, as I have already hinted, to separate them from each other. The concept of the individual here employed is a psychological one. It is assumed that each person is made up of psychic functions which are in part everywhere the same, i.e. collective; they are also unique in every respect, just as everybody has finger-prints but each of these is unique in the formation of the actual elements. Thus, each person is at once collective and individual. Because of the individuality, each person is absolutely separated from every other; the degree of separation may be very small or very great, but it is always there. The concept *individual* differs essentially from that of *personal*, which involves the question of relationships between the conscious minds of two or more people, together with the repressed, and so unconscious, personal material deriving from the early years of development onwards. In this paper, personal is used in the above sense and does not indicate the conception of the whole integrated personality which is termed the *self*.

In spite of these concepts we can build an illusory distinction between individual and collective responses. I would like to give an example from my own experience of the kind of illusion that can come from this division. When the fall of France occurred in 1940, I had a feeling which ran as follows: 'Thank heaven, now there is nobody to let us down.' Now that might be considered as my own piece of private insanity; in point of fact, however, it was a frequent reaction, even, I am told on good authority which I am unable to quote, the commonest statistical response. I had therefore experienced as an individual a collective or mass reaction. As an individual it was possible for me to avoid identification with the collective response and to have other ideas about it—for instance I inquired from my refugee friends how the Nazis treated doctors and then gradually arrived at a more balanced judgement.

If one of these collective reactions gets loose from the individual, then it becomes uncontrollable, and it is therefore more than important for the individual to know how to handle these responses. Let us suppose that I had been one of a meeting predisposed to a collective response. A speaker expressing 'Thank heaven, now there is nobody to let us down' in suitably colourful language, would have aroused latent emotions in each person and in spite of himself he would be more or less carried away, losing perhaps his real individual judgement altogether. Only afterwards, when on his own, would doubts start to assemble themselves. If each person was functioning as an individual in the imaginary meeting, then there would be no emotion which would carry the audience off its feet. The essential difference between the two kinds of response by the group depends upon the degree of coherence which each individual is able to attain. This means the degree to which the psychic elements are built into an 'inner world' of psychic functions, and this depends upon the existence of the individuality, for if each person was identical with his fellows there would be no means of separating one from the other.

The value contained in the 'inner world' depends upon the extent to which the individual is able to recognize and bear the conflict of opposites invariably accompanied by the feeling of suffering which we must consequently regard as a significant element in our psychic life. If the individual is not sufficiently coherent to stand the tension, he can deal with one of the opposites by projecting it. According to our social psychic organization, our culture pattern, he is supported by general approval if he projects the element of evil which, because it is primitive and undifferentiated by neglect, is something to be fought with all the means in his power. This is the psychic basis for outbreaks of war. Our role as analysts in the prevention of war must therefore be to do all we can to make the individual conscious of the collective (archetypal) affects which he contains, and to work out ways of solving intolerable conflicts.

Jung,[7] referring to Society and State as examples of massed individuals, says:

Society or the State derive their quality from the individual's mental condition, for they are constituted by individuals. . . . No matter how obvious this fact is, it has not yet permeated collective opinion sufficiently for people to refrain from using the term 'State' as if it referred to a sort of super-individual endowed with inexhaustible power and resourcefulness.

It is worth reflecting on why the term 'State' is made into a 'sort of super-individual' and I would like to put forward the following proposition: it has grown out of man's yearning to be

[7] *Essays on Contemporary Events*, p. xvii.

freed from individual responsibility towards the conflict of opposites, and this is why he projects his individuality into the State.
I base this proposition upon the idea that where there is a projection we find the belief in an overwhelming power for good or
evil, without any good idea of how this power is to work, or what
that power is. The result of projecting the individuality is to
open the way for the masses—which constitute the nation—to
become collective and unconscious.

Turning to the history of the crisis in our society, there is
general agreement that it started many years ago, long before the
wars with Germany. Dr. Bion considers it in relation to the year
1907 for reasons of his own, but it has clearly been going on far
longer than that. The gradual disintegration of the standard of
values which our institutions uphold could equally well be
dated from the end of the Middle Ages, since there has been no
dominant authority in the Western hemisphere since the Roman
Catholic Church began to disintegrate. Instead moral standards
have gradually fragmented and in consequence have become
more and more relative, until finally we arrive at the position
when a considerable group of individuals discovers that it does
not know what the crisis means, while others take up the position
that values are the concern of individuals only.

As psychologists, we investigate psychic states. There are some
people who prefer not to know the nature of the crisis, but there
are others who like to feel they have a solution. Inasmuch as
there is no single answer which finds general acceptance, there
has grown up a regular babel of voices which we might label a
'lunatic' state of affairs, after Dr. Bion. To say that the present
causes of the crisis are unknown means, from the psychological
point of view, that we approach the matter with that attitude—
a good one for research purposes. By way of contrast there are
others, for instance those who are thoroughly contained in
Christianity, who know the solution.

But it does not seem to me useful to refer, as Dr. Bion does, to
the present state of the world as 'lunatic', except in connection
with the babel of voices. I recognize that in so doing he expresses
a collective attitude towards current events which we find particularly amongst those who want the human race to carry on its
affairs on the basis of intelligence and good sense. But this has
never occurred for more than very brief periods, and is unlikely

to occur in the near future, because irrational, primitive and trans-personal forces always tend to dominate in critical periods. The word 'lunatic' is not a good one because it is too often used to undervalue a particular state of affairs which contains positive as well as negative potentialities.

In pointing to the beginning of decay in the Roman Catholic Church as the origin of the crisis, I intend to suggest that it comes about through the decay of institutions which hold the dominating position in any society, because they contain the distilled wisdom of man, organized and brought firmly into consciousness through the labour of centuries. Institutions represent the collective consciousness of mankind and, though they express some aspects of the unconscious within them by means of ritual, they have tended to avoid bringing this home as a psychological function. Yet well-rooted institutions can show their vitality in the capacity to develop and absorb new ideas and movements which grow up outside their confines and, in recent years, we have witnessed education, the law, and religious bodies gradually assimilating psychological concepts.

As psychologists we have been inclined to disregard our institutions, i.e. the conscious functions, in favour of the more fascinating problems which the unconscious provides. This tendency can be discerned in Dr. Bion's paper; he pays scant attention to them, and I smell a tendency to underestimate their capacity for dealing with human problems; moreover he appears to overlook important realities about them, so that one cannot help reflecting that he might well apply some energy in fact-finding to them. For instance, it is untrue that our religious and political institutions do not deal with unconscious motivation or, should we not rather say, do not deal with elements of the unconscious. The Church deals elaborately with parent/child relationships in their symbolical aspect; an exhaustive imagery of the Mother and the Father and the Child, whilst there is no doubt that the imagery of the self is also represented in the Church ritual of the Mass.[8] In addition, very far-reaching investigations

---

[8] The argument upon which this statement is based is taken from Jung. It is far too difficult and complicated a research to summarize here, and the reader must be referred to the original paper, 'Transformation Symbolism in the Mass', *Psychology and Religion: West and East* (Collected Works, Vol. XI). London and New York, 1958.

into human psychology have been carried out by smaller religious communities, even though we may regard them as inadequate from our position. My own investigations into Catholic mysticism have, for instance, taught me that St. John of the Cross[9] was able to describe quite distinctly many phenomena of the unconscious which have been discovered by Freud and Jung. One can easily see such phenomena as fixation to the breast, the feeling of frustration and anger at separation from it and the negative transference from Freud's work; the soul is without doubt identical with Jung's description of the anima.

Therefore it seems likely that our institutions might well provide us with very considerable information about how to handle groups and also about what is necessary for their organization. The following statement by the Deputy Speaker, which provided considerable food for thought, appeared in *The Times*.[10] It consisted of his saying: 'It is out of order to attribute motives to an individual member, but it is not out of order to attribute motives to a party.' Parliament is an organization with much experience behind it, and a ruling of that kind would not be made without very good reason. There are two points which occur to me: one is that a party is more intangible than an individual, and so the question of motive can be swamped and the guilt, if any, of it is shared amongst its members. To pick out an individual immediately isolates him from the collective, and that has to be avoided, especially as it may reveal the inferior personal motive in a collective situation. But, when this has been said, the ruling introduces us to the subject of collective guilt,[11] which it would be wrong to take as a personal responsibility. From this position to impute motives to an individual member opens the door to scapegoat psychology and so, owing to the projection of the group, the individual might wrongly be made responsible for the collective guilt of the party.

When Dr. Bion points out that our institutions fall back before criticism of their attitude to personal and unconscious motivation, and while this is true, we need to realize that any large

[9] See 'Dark Night of the Soul', below.

[10] *The Times*. House of Commons debate on the coal shortage, Saturday, 8 February 1947, p. 8, col. 3.

[11] For further elaboration of this theme, cf. Jung, 'After the Catastrophe', *Essays on Contemporary Events*. London, 1947, pp. 45 ff.

organization inevitably collects together a number of people who join it for the wrong motive. There is no way of changing this thoroughly negative situation, except by undertaking the gigantic task of improving the quality of individuals. The dynamic state of society necessitates the continuous assimilation of new elements from the collective unconscious. Since institutions represent what is known to work, they resist innovations; this they are bound to do if they are going to maintain their position. Institutions are always behind the times, always conservative, so that they will always be out of date, and liable to fair criticism from those who are 'modern men'.[12] From this aspect they are always inadequate. Yet their relation to new developments, connected in an essential way with the individual, represents an important element in the dynamics of change, for in being conservative they maintain connection with the transpersonal psyche.

Without doubt the transpersonal attitude of individuals in groups is emphasized again and again. In the Church the Priest is essentially transpersonal. Until recently Royalty spoke of themselves in public as 'we'. Though leaders nowadays call themselves 'I', they are, none the less, thoroughly transpersonal and can become only mythological figures.[13] In recent years particularly Lenin and Hitler have been placed in this position by the Russians and Germans respectively. Let me, finally, quote from the Chairman's address. He says: 'I hope that my impartiality as Chairman will not be put in doubt . . .' He therefore implicitly recognizes the transpersonal function which it is necessary for him to fulfil; one has to respect 'the Chair' which its occupant represents.[14]

In reading Dr. Bion's very subtly, and on the whole, cautiously

---

[12] Cf. p. 22 f. above.

[13] The substitution of 'I' for 'we' is a significant event, inasmuch as the personality of the king or leader comes more into the open. It occurs to me that this is a symptom of a general trend in the assimilation of unconscious contents. The king, if it be a king, is no longer simply a function but a person performing that function.

[14] Impartiality is not to be identified with the transpersonal, but it seems to me impossible to be impartial if personal feelings are allowed to come into the picture. The Chairman has in reality no name, he for the time being loses his own identity completely and becomes what can only be described as a transpersonal function holding the scales of justice, as it were, in his hand.

worded paper, I do not find that sufficient attention is paid to the fact that a group organizes itself on this transpersonal basis; in fact, he is much more concerned to show that the question of personal relationships is the important factor in a group. But personal relationships are of critical importance in small groups only, perhaps we should say only amongst their leaders, and it is impossible to take personal considerations into account when handling larger groups because they function at much more archaic levels and obey the dictates, not of individual and personal, but of collective psychology. But even so, collective phenomena can be observed in a relatively small group and Dr. Bion has observed one of them, without however drawing the essential conclusions. He has generously given us his own experience which can therefore be quoted from his paper. He observed an occupational therapy department and says about it:

'. . . it seemed to me that some kind of equilibrium had been achieved by community and patients alike, and that the nature of the equilibrium was not even observed, leave alone understood. My suspicions were confirmed when in hospital I tried to make a group of patients aware of the nature of their afflictions as an object of study by the group. . . . The emotional volcano blew its head off and, as luck would have it, I was deposited at a point from which I could watch the clouds of smoke and dust with a certain amount of detachment and serious interest.[15]

This type of reaction must be common knowledge, but its significance can only be grasped by the individual who alone possesses the consciousness to do it, i.e. Dr. Bion, as an individual, 'could watch . . . with a certain amount of detachment and serious interest.'

Mass reactions happen in an uncontrolled, a transpersonal and unconscious way. In my experience in dealing with evacuation problems during World War II, one could not rely on a group of either children or villagers remaining anywhere near stable; it vacillated in its allegiance constantly and within very wide bounds. Behind this uncertainty there lay the mass reactions, which overrode individual and personal considerations and depended upon primitive moral standards. This will be made clearer by an example. During evacuation, the inhabitants of a village invariably reacted in a typical way when three groups of

[15] These quotations were taken from the typescript of Dr. Bion's paper and do not correspond exactly with the published version.

phenomena came to their notice amongst evacuees: sexual activities, destructiveness, and delinquency. The ideas which they expressed were those of more or less violent moral disapproval along the lines made known to us by Freud as those coming from the super-ego. It is a familiar fact that if these outraged individuals are analysed many contents of the personal unconscious can be discerned, and once these are made conscious the super-ego pattern is modified. But this does not explain the immediate, total, transpersonal and fundamentally unconscious reaction which has merely been depotentiated rather than removed.

Turning to another field than evacuation or Dr. Bion's observations—when France fell, even *The Times* descended to mythological projection. Hitler became the serpent who 'covers with slime the body of its prospective victim.'[16] The war provided us with more evidence, if it were needed, in Mr. Churchill's speeches, where all the English hatred of tyranny, of oppression, was mobilized. We have only to look at parliamentary elections and politics to see the value of slogans, whilst the main apparatus of religion deals in 'supernatural' transpersonal archetypal forms.

I have dwelt on this subject because it leads on to the problem of psychiatric disinheritance, a subject which easily catches our sympathy since the disinherited persons are fewer in number and therefore often need protection against the mass and transpersonal judgements of society. Dr. Bion's unwillingness to define what this disinheritance involves is most understandable, but the question is so pressing that someone is bound to say something about it. In general terms the disinherited are those people who do not fit satisfactorily into our social institutions; they cannot be contained in the various groups and organizations which society provides. It is the function of our institutions to contain, organize, or hold in check mass phenomena which are projected into them. Inasmuch as they do this they perform their main function and so take the burden of consciousness off the individual. But inasmuch as they do not succeed, the collective phenomena (i.e. the archetypes of the collective unconscious) return to the individual. This places upon him an increased psychological burden—some can stand it, others cannot. Some become, if they are not so already, patently pathological, and so

16 *The Times*. Leading article: 'Against Treachery', 23 May 1940.

we can at least hold off the problem to some extent by giving them a long word (a diagnosis!) by way of consolation, or by removing them to an asylum—I use this word in its original sense, not referring only to the Mental Hospital. Others can be returned to society; but others of them are by no means only abnormal, they are exceptional individuals, potentially capable of withstanding the clash of opposites, referred to above, in the inner world. Because of this, the problem is not one which we can hand over to the administrator, since it has a deeper significance for us, striking right at the core of our sense of values and leading to the extremely thorny question of the way in which we cure or do not cure our patients. Each person who is disinherited has a chance of becoming conscious of the opposites to an unusual degree and so of becoming especially valuable to society; that must not be overlooked.

Each person who is submitted to a therapeutic manœuvre has to submit to a valuation by the psychiatrist, who has to decide whether the aim of his treatment should be the limited one of fitting him into the social system, or whether his individuality is an essential feature of his problem; that means, whether he has to support the individual in his refusal to submit to collective criteria.[17] The task of individuation—for it is this to which I refer—involves isolation and disinheritance, but it should lead back to a creative contribution to society in one form or another. Such a patient will only be injured by an attempt to force him into a mould and in the end, society will be the loser. It is unclear how many patients fall into this class, but even if it be only a few, they should not be overlooked on any account.

Where our organizations are weak is in the relation to individual differences, but how they can be expected to do more than tolerate them is not clear without adopting and developing psychological techniques. With these they could assist their members in their personal relationships and so remove a factor which is apt to crop up in group discord. But even if these were well handled the capacity to understand collective issues is limited and will always be so, especially as they become more complex and technical. In consequence the majority of our

[17] Cf. Fordham, 'A Comparative Study between the Effects of Analysis and Electrical Convulsion Therapy in a case of Schizophrenia', *British Journal of Medical Psychology*, Vol. XX, 1946, p. 412.

society will always be the prey to prejudices and these can be manipulated by the minority of so-called leaders.[18] Our contribution should be, therefore, to induce people to interest themselves in their own capacity for conscious understanding—'the eyes of the fool are on the ends of the earth'. As in the analysis of individuals we start gradually with personal and more manageable conflicts, so in handling the group we should start from comparable phenomena, leaving the institutions to deal with the collective phenomena; that is what they are framed to do, and we can learn from them so long as they fulfil their function within the limits defined above, only offering our interpretations as contributions towards failures as they come sufficiently near consciousness.

In periods of bewilderment like the present, we can usefully offer interpretations as Dr. Bion has done. He considers the important factor in the rise and fall of civilizations to be the cohesive capacity of the group which is based on personal relationships: 'if a man cannot be friends with his friends, he cannot be an enemy to his enemies' (ibid., p. 88). This statement is incomplete not only for the reasons we have considered, but also because groups do not for long cohere in purposive activity without a leader. The leader often comes from amongst disinherited individuals; one can readily think of a good many examples.[19] Therefore how society treats its outcasts is also an important item. The potentially creative outcast is the potential individual; creative leadership comes out of the individual and not out of the masses.

Applying this idea to medical psychology: it is how we treat our failures which is the most important factor in its future development.

Let us now turn to the problem of how we deal with our enemies, for outcasts can become enemies. This is another pressing problem, since these enemies are apparently liable to get too real, and we have seen how the worst situation can arise in Germany, when the outcasts become in fantasy the enemies of society.[20] I take it that by the psychologically trained reader it

[18] Cf. Jung, *Essays on Contemporary Events.* London, 1947.

[19] For example, Lenin, Freud, and Jung. Churchill obviously also, but only in a mitigated form.

[20] This situation is likely to die down in our country as the 'blood lust' of war gets depotentiated.

will be understood if I say that our concern is with them as unassimilated psychic factors; analytical psychology defines them under the heading of the *shadow*.

The vague term 'shadow' is chosen because it gives an image to unconscious functioning which is in the last resort indeterminate. It also expresses the animistic tendency of unconscious functions. The shadow is the image through which psychic inferiorities, difficult to assimilate because of the guilt frequently associated with them, can find expression.[21] It is usually at first projected on to somebody else. In the example I gave earlier, the French had come to represent the shadow, the inferior function of a large mass of the English people. During the 1914–18 war, it may be remembered, there was a tendency to make the French the scapegoat for military reverses. Indeed, in history, as well as today, the French have tended to constellate the English shadow, and vice versa.

It is difficult enough to assimilate the shadow in its personal aspect, but it is far more difficult in the case of a group, because it becomes more primitive and much less manageable, so that once it gains momentum there is no stopping it; little or no sense of self-preservation remains.

The problem of assimilating the shadow is one of our time. Religion has attempted to deal with it symbolically in demonology, but it has not been successful, to our cost. It has been taken up, as Zilboorg and Henry have shown in *History of Medical Psychology*,[22] by psycho-analysis, but has found its most significant handling in Jung's 'Answer to Job'.[23]

The shadow is the special field of medical psychology and we pay for this in our public relations and internal conflicts, but we know more about it than anybody else and consequently we have an obligation to present it to the community in such a way that it can be digested. This has been done with a certain success, but it is a difficult undertaking because there is a tendency for us to get shadow projections in return for our efforts. This must clearly be expected, since we are showing up the inferiorities of the

---

[21] The term shadow though implying valuation is not to be taken in a moral sense. The concept is morally neutral. From a moral point of view the contents of the shadow may be good or bad, but ultimately it is neither. Hence Jung's definition of it as the 'natural man'.

[22] New York, 1941.   [23] *Psychology and Religion: West and East.*

institutions. The projection comes about through the tendency of inferiorities to be identified with evil which must be rejected by a community which needs to maintain sufficient sense of being good. We know how hard the process is in the case of individuals; it is far harder with a small group and harder still when we come to the mass of humanity—indeed, I judge it to be impossible. Just imagine what would happen if the Archbishop of Canterbury made it obligatory for a day to be set aside for the worship of the Devil according to a scientifically constructed ritual worked out by the British Psychological Society!

The general interest in crime and the public concern over the decay of morals is overwhelming evidence in support of Dr. Bion's and Dr. Rickman's idea that the community needs '. . . to gain insight into the psychological origin of at least some part, and in my [Dr. Bion's] opinion a major part of its distress.'[24] But, if we try to do this, it is vitally important to evaluate the positive aspects of the institutions upon which society is founded. If the bulk of the community do not feel them to be sufficiently good, violent revolutionary movements will be set on foot; that is the main reason why I criticize Dr. Bion's somewhat casual reference to them. I may perhaps be allowed to comment that Jung's attempt to perform an interpretative function for the Nazi movement resulted on the one hand in his being put on the Nazi black-list, and on the other, accused of being either in sympathy with the Nazis or actually being one himself; this he must have expected as a consequence of his attempt. He has recently attempted the same for our distress in his broadcast talk 'The Fight with the Shadow'[25] with quite different results—it was acceptable. Though our community is not so unstable as Germany was, the danger of interpreting the community's distress is that we simply get disregarded, ostracized, or passively accepted —each is equally unstable. If, on the other hand, we can find the right attitude starting from ourselves, then, being secure in our group functioning, we can venture on a wider field.

This leads on to the consideration of how to approach collective psychology. In many ways, the group is not a good unit to start from, but especially because the larger it grows, the more primitive and uncontrollable it tends to become when archetypal

[24] Bion, ibid.
[25] Cf. Jung, *Essays on Contemporary Events*. London, 1947.

contents are constellated. It is certainly possible to dig deeper in individual cases, but criteria are required to know when mass or collective phenomena begin to emerge if we are attempting to estimate group reactions in the individual.[26] This can be done by considering the individual as a function of the society in which he lives and differentiating his personal problems from the collective attitudes of which he is a part. This is easy if what is produced be common knowledge, i.e. part of the collective conscious. When, however, phenomena come from the collective unconscious they require amplification in order to recognize them.

This research on collective psychology begins with individuals and can be related to the literature and observed behaviour of natural groups such as nations.

In approaching the matter thus, we can not only go deeper, but we also find that history, philosophy, art, and religion spring to life before our eyes as psychic processes living in the present.[27] Dr. Bion's fascinating use of historical research gains from being looked at in this way. As I understand his use of the material he is approaching it from *without* inwards; he views history as an external phenomenon of the past from which we can draw conclusions about the present external situation to which man has to relate himself. We may, however, look at history as a projection of the collective psyche into the past, and I am more inclined by temperament to do this, i.e. to start from *within* outwards. These two attitudes are by no means antagonistic, they are indeed reciprocal and can be useful to each other; by looking inwards we can throw light on the outer situation and by looking outwards we can throw light on the inner processes.

Looking at history as a projection makes it easier to apply comparative methods. As I thought about Toynbee's analysis of the rise and fall of civilization, the rise of an oppressive dominant minority and the final attempt of the masses to save its soul,[28] I

[26] Historically the problem has been approached in this way: psychotherapy has spent some fifty years in studying individuals and only more recently has the attempt been made to apply the knowledge so gained to group psychotherapy.

[27] I am here following Freud in asserting that psychology is a central science round which other sciences and humanities could group themselves.

[28] The soul, according to analytical psychology, has a specific function, namely of mediating between the ego and the unconscious, just in the

was irresistibly reminded of the *Gilgamish Epic*,[29] which dates from about 2000 B.C., in which we find the same theme, though couched in very different terms. This epic is concerned with the King of Erech, Gilgamish, whose rule became so oppressive that the people, i.e. the masses, prayed to the sky god, Anu. In reply the goddess Aruru was instructed to make a 'fellow' to Gilgamish so that the two shall strive together and so 'unto Erech give surcease'. The myth relates that a conflict takes place, resulting in a friendship from which Gilgamish gains strength. The common factor in the myth and in Toynbee's analysis is the oppressive minority and the attempt of the masses to save themselves. In the Gilgamish Epic a solution is brought about through the friendship of Enkidu and Gilgamish and a different state of stability is arrived at.[30] I reflected that the essential principle had been expressed rather a long time ago and that the problem had not changed much throughout the ages. But though the principle had been understood in the past in various ways, this was not adequate for our period. The different interpretations of an essential theme vary from age to age and are concerned with the development of consciousness; can we not safely take modern psychology as a part of that development?

At this point it does not seem to me valuable to go further into causes, but following Jung, to look at the matter in terms of meaning and aim. What then does it mean that man has attempted to develop a scientific psychology and under what circumstances is it likely to be of importance? In this connection Dr. Bion's reflections about the significance of technical developments which, in producing leisure, tend to liberate previously unconscious forces, come to the fore. Technical developments tend to

same way as the persona mediates between the ego and the external world. Since the masses reveal the collective, in Toynbee's situation they will reveal the collective unconscious. The collective unconscious does not possess a soul in the sense of anima.

[29] R. C. Thompson (trans.), *The Epic of Gilgamish*. London, 1928.

[30] The psychological analysis of this myth is fertile ground for the problems of our era. The friendship of Gilgamish for Enkidu, the primitive natural man, is initiated by the Hatiera who teaches him and introduces him to civilization. Through their intercourse Enkidu is estranged from his natural life. This incident brings forward the importance of woman's role in the transformation of primitive impulses—a modern problem.

do something other than producing leisure, however; they produce an orderly state of affairs in the external world so that the disorderly elements which lay there before become introjected, causing a state of internal unrest, and man himself is realized as the source of dangerous disorder. For this reason we hear over and over again 'Will *man* be able to control the powers which he has unleashed from nature?' This reflection gives a powerful motive for the study of the psyche. Man is, indeed, becoming aware of himself, of his own helpless and infantile consciousness, so that we have to ask 'What is the significance of our crisis in terms of man?'[31]

Since the Middle Ages we have witnessed a process which may be regarded as the progressive removal of projections from the external world, from the skies, from the earth and from matter. This has been largely due to the development of natural science which has given us an enormously greater knowledge of, and control over, the material world. But the removal of projections does not deal with their energy content. The energy simply sinks back to its original source, namely man himself, where it piles up and threatens his conscious world more and more. Sooner or later a critical state of affairs must arise in which the conscious values become threatened with total destruction unless something can be done to understand their significance, to interpret them and develop a new conscious orientation.

Before the war the individual was getting increasingly into the grasp of large organizations and felt himself powerless in the face of them; in addition he was—and this applies even more today, as Dr. Bion points out—bombarded with problems and decisions which moved him emotionally, but to which he could make no direct response. Life began to lack meaning and significance, and a kind of apathetic, indifferent, helpless attitude was common. These phenomena all indicate a lowered threshold of consciousness; the old values of the past were wearing out.

This negative state carries with it the consequence, since the unconscious compensates the conscious mind, that libido is sinking into the unconscious where it raises the energy potential in the archetypes. Sooner or later this energy in the unconscious is bound to threaten the conscious mind. It was certainly beginning

[31] The following interpretation is almost entirely taken from Jung's work, cf. *Essays on Contemporary Events*, et al.

to do so before the war, but the conflict with Germany provided an opportunity to re-establish our traditional position, i.e. our collective consciousness—freedom, democracy, the rights of man in the political sphere and Christianity in the religious sphere— over against Germany, which came to represent the forces in the collective unconscious—according to Jung, the old god 'Wotan' —against which every resistance in our power was raised. It would be a mistake to assume that the conflict is over because the war has ended, and for this reason it is not surprising to find that the conflict and difficulties do not subside, that the crisis goes on, and that scarcely anybody expects it to be otherwise.

If we are to grasp what the phenomena going on in Germany mean to us, we have to consider what happened there as we saw it. In the main, Germany provided us with a warning of what monstrous barbarity man is capable of if he becomes possessed by ideals. But if we are to apply our knowledge to the management of an eruption from the unconscious a certain modicum of im- partial objectivity is essential.

Two phenomena from the midst of all the monstrous barbarity stand out as ambivalent: the new order and the race of supermen. The new order was the fantasy of a planned economy enforced from above. We can see that clearly enough: the danger of a flight into order away from conflict—the danger of deluding ourselves into making a robot civilization. The conflict is actually stated in the religious and political terms of relationship between, on the one hand, the traditional value of the individual based on Chris- tianity, and on the other, a planned economy tending to a totali- tarian system. Dr. Bion's reference to the trades unions as pro- viding the workers with a restoration of their lost inheritance must be qualified by saying that they are also in danger of being devoured by the powerful and potentially dangerous forces of order: the identification of the individual with them is perhaps the main threat of the moment.

At the same time the idea of planning contains the positive effort of man towards controlling his destiny, but in order to function it must be handled by man so that he does not become the instrument of his plan. The solution may be clear enough in individual cases, but its issue is only begun on the collective or social plane and the outcome is by no means decided.

The spectacle of the British Empire divesting itself of the usual accoutrements of power involves an inward turning movement. In order to be effective, this movement must be accompanied by an increase in consciousness, or else disintegration will threaten us according to Toynbee's model. What is that new element of consciousness? Perhaps it is concerned with the superman theme which the Germans caricatured, and which Jung has interpreted as follows. When speaking of the present situation and the future, he says:[32]

The value and importance of the individual are rapidly decreasing and the chances of his being heard will vanish more and more. This process of deterioration will be long and painful, but I am afraid it is inevitable. Yet in the long run it will prove to be the only way by which man's lamentable unconsciousness, his childishness and individual weakness can be replaced by a future man, who knows that he himself is the maker of his fate, and that the State is his tool and not his master.

In Dr. Bion's concluding paragraph we find (p. 89):

Whether our country, of all countries, is capable of meeting the challenge of our time will only be determined by what we ourselves do.

Is that the voice of the new man?

In ending on a speculative note I hope nobody will think the archetype of the new man is in itself new. On the contrary, it is as old as history, appearing in different forms in each age. The form which it takes in our time is psychological and this opens up new possibilities. We only speculate when we consider whether it will come into the general consciousness of mankind, or whether it will remain a myth.

[32] *Essays on Contemporary Events*, p. xiii.

VIII

ANALYTICAL PSYCHOLOGY AND RELIGIOUS EXPERIENCE[1]

THERE can be no doubt that the concept of the collective unconscious has made a considerable impact on religious thought and has added a new facet to the study of religious experience. It has achieved so much because it mediates between belief in metaphysical reality and psychological theory, between religious practices and psychological analysis.

It could be, and indeed has been, maintained that the observations on which Jung's theory is based reveal nothing new, in that they have been known and recorded since the dawn of history; but even if this be conceded, his approach is new. It differs from that of theologians in at least one essential respect: theologians are at liberty to hold that the primordial images are revelations deriving from an objective reality extending beyond the human psyche to which psychologists are restricted. They also go further and claim that psychologists should limit themselves to a psyche as conceived by them and so restrict analytical psychologists in ways they consider justifiable. Sometimes the theologians' argument excludes the manifest psychological content of images as if Jung's concept had never been formulated. Before then they were indeed on secure grounds in confining psychology within the bounds of personal experience. Since the introduction of Jung's concept this can no longer be done.

There is, however, no logical incompatibility between the two different viewpoints if the phenomena are recognized as common to each discipline which treats them differently. If the two fields of knowledge get mixed up, this is only to be expected, for it is

[1] First read to the Guild of Pastoral Psychology, and published as *Guild Lecture No. 46*, Guild of Pastoral Psychology Pamphlet, March 1947. It has been revised.

clear that psychology must lead sooner or later to religious experience, while religion can only be brought home to the individual through the psyche. In spite of this Jung, and so analytical psychology as a whole, has been attacked for psychologism, i.e. the belief that religion is only psychology. This criticism would seem to spring from the fear that psychology will in the end dispense with religion. There is little hope of reassuring the critics by logical treatment, for it springs only in part from ignorance of the nature of psychological methodology; for the rest it is an affective and so irrational fear on the part of religious people. In his defence Jung has pointed out that though physicists have reduced matter to energy this does not dispense with matter for most purposes; no more need psychology dispense with religion. Most natural sciences assume that the material world, whether it be conceived in terms of energy or not, is an objective datum, their methodology depends upon it; but analysis of perception leads to the conclusion that the existence of material objects is wholly inferred from a perceptual image constructed by the brain in relation to the psyche. This conclusion does not have much influence on the physical sciences in question.

The problem of overlapping springs to view if it be assumed that we can distinguish between a religious person and an organized religious body. Not much good, for the present purpose, can come from trying to define a religious person, but we may all agree about him when we see him. He may or may not belong to a religious body and he need not even profess formal religious beliefs; some scientists are religious people, and science even follows the religious spirit in its quest for truth, but it has no formal religious creed. Indeed, it differs from formal religion in most respects.

When we come to the organized religious body or system, we at once meet clearly defined phenomena. These are: (1) The belief through faith in the metaphysical reality of God, which is taken to be proved by reason and a number of miraculous supernatural events; (2) Ritual exercises, confession, prayers, services; and (3) Spiritual experiences, which in the mystical communities are highly developed. These take the form of visions and dreams, or, on the highest plane, a fundamentally indefinable sublime experience of God, the *unio mystica*.

Certain of these phenomena can be treated as psychological,

particularly those in the second and most of those in the third category. The first category, that of the metaphysical reality of God, cannot be grasped by psychology, though such miraculous proofs as the virgin birth are accessible to psychological examination.

At first sight doubts may well be lulled to rest. Religion depends upon faith in the transcendental reality of God, and rests upon a kind of reality which transcends every experience. Religion, in particular theology, looks at the phenomena from its metaphysical position and comes to conclusions about the nature of God; psychology looks at them from the theory of the collective unconscious and comes to conclusions about human nature.

Unfortunately for this division most analysts, though not all, are quite satisfied with their experience and do not care about the transcendental reality which can only be known through faith. They usually gain support for this indifference because of the extraordinary abuses to which faith opens the door.

It may seem regrettable that many psychologists simply do not care about belief, but we have to remember that many of them regard themselves as religious people on the ground that they claim to know about religious experiences out of which they form an individual philosophy of life. Psychologists may conclude with certainty that a genuine religious attitude can exist without belief in an historical miracle and without philosophical proof; but that attitude is not accessible to scientific investigation as such, it can only be the subject-matter of psychology. Therefore, though a psychologist may be a religious person, as a psychologist he must regard his religious experience in an objective light. If he identifies himself with his experience, then, whatever may be the other gains, he is lost to psychology.

In the past the archetypal images arising from the collective unconscious have been understood as only a religious reality. Thus, though the soul had a psychological reference, its main importance was in relation to the dogma of its survival after death. It was merely clothed in a body for a brief sojourn on earth, and only during this period could its phenomena become accessible to psychology. Psychology, however, must be subject to biological criteria, and so the soul without a body is of no interest. The soul's religious significance cannot be embraced by psychological means and the belief in its survival can only be grasped through interpretation. If we do interpret the belief in the soul's survival, we conclude that it indicates the extraordinarily high value, the *numinosum*, which is attributed to that organ of the unconscious psyche. When this is done we are, however, outside traditional religion completely and it follows that there can be no psychology of religion, only a psychology of religious phenomena.

A religious position can lay claim to absolute knowledge about God, and consequently to knowledge of what really constitutes good and evil. Therefore, if its basic concepts be accepted, it has an absolute right to wield authority on spiritual and moral issues. Analytical psychology, on the contrary, can only take up an individual and relative position in relation to religious values, since any authority which it possesses is derived from knowledge based upon accumulated experience with human beings. Its authority is based on the standards of its empirical scientific approach.

From what has been said it will be clear that the methodology of theology and that of psychology are different. To the psychologist the religious commentaries on biblical and mystical texts may, but do not necessarily, contain much that is of interest because of their completely different presuppositions. It therefore appears at the present stage in the development of our young science, that a psychologist is quite within his rights if he ignores much religious and theological literature which to the complementary discipline would be essential. It is even desirable that he do so, since otherwise he attempts to understand a complex field of study in which he has not trained. If my remarks in this and the following two essays appear naive to those with a more thorough education in religion than I possess, I can only crave their indulgence.

RELIGIOUS RITUAL

The main collective religious experience is contained in the ritual. This seems much more useful to take as a starting point than those mass religious possessions which sometimes occur in evangelical circles. In this paper I will confine myself in the main to Christianity, because that is the religious milieu in which we live and also the basis on which pastoral psychology can thrive.

There had been no detailed study of Christian rituals by any analytical psychologist till Professor Jung's recent research into the Mass.[2] I propose to take some aspects of his work as a basis for discussion, especially since the Mass stands at the centre of Christian ritual observances. As I read a part of Jung's paper I was at once struck by the way in which his analysis brought me right to the central theme of Christian mysticism as expressed in the work of St. John of the Cross, whose *The Dark Night of the Soul* had occupied my attention for some time past. The Mass is a collective event, while the mystical experience is highly individual, so that a comparative study will be likely to produce results germane to our subject.

Let us turn to some relevant passages from Jung's work. He says:[3]

The Church's view [of the Mass] therefore presupposes the following psychological situation: human consciousness (represented by the priest and congregation) is confronted with an autonomous event which, taking place on a 'divine' and 'timeless' plane transcending consciousness, is in no way dependent on human action, but which impels man to act by seizing upon him as an instrument and making him the exponent of a 'divine' happening. In the ritual action man places himself at the disposal of an autonomous and 'eternal' agency operating outside the categories of human consciousness—*si parva licet componere magnis* —in much the same way that a good actor does not merely represent the drama, but allows himself to be overpowered by the genius of the dramatist.

And again:[4]

The ordinary man cannot find anything in himself that would cause him to perform a 'mystery'. He can only do so if and when *it* seizes upon *him*. This seizure, or rather the sensed or presumed existence of a power outside consciousness which seizes him, is the miracle par excellence, really and truly a miracle when one considers *what* is being represented.

According to Jung, the Mass is a self-dedication. The confession before the ritual has the aim of giving up or clearing out all egoistic motives, so that the sacrifice of the ego to the divine mystery, the central theme of the Mass, may be complete. In the

[2] 'Transformation Symbolism in the Mass', *Psychology and Religion: West and East* (Collected Works, Vol. XI). London and New York, 1958.
[3] p. 249.   [4] p. 250.

rite the congregation actually offer themselves to God, taking God into themselves and so becoming one with God. In doing this they paradoxically strengthen themselves:[5]

... since the gift represents myself, I have in that case destroyed myself, given myself away without expectation of return. Yet, looked at in another way, this intentional loss is also a gain, for if you can give yourself it proves that you possess yourself. Nobody can give what he has not got.

In consequence the Mass is an act of integration. The whole ritual is carried out with the aid of material objects and is performed by the priest in the church. This is inevitable in such a ritual because the unconscious mind has to be projected and needs drama into which to project its contents.

THE INDIVIDUAL EXPERIENCE

Let us now turn to the individual experience embodied in Christian mysticism, and take note of some passages from *The Dark Night of the Soul* by St. John of the Cross. This work is of particular interest to a psychologist because of its objective, detailed, empirical and even 'clinical' approach to the whole problem. Moreover, St. John quite clearly describes many phenomena familiar to analysts through their practical work.

The Dark Night of the Soul is an account of phases in mystical development. There are three stages: That of the Beginners, that of the First Dark Night, and that of the Second Dark Night.

The stage of the Beginners revolves round a central theme which may be grasped from the following quotation:[6]

It must be known, then, that the soul, after it has been definitely converted to the service of God, is, as a rule, spiritually nurtured and caressed by God, even as is the tender child by its loving mother, who warms it with the heat of her bosom and nurtures it with sweet milk and soft and pleasant food, and carries it and caresses it in her arms; but, as the child grows bigger, the mother gradually ceases caressing it, and, hiding her tender love, puts bitter aloes upon her sweet breast, sets down the child from her arms and makes it walk upon its feet, so that it may lose the characteristics of a child and betake itself to greater and more substantial occupations.

[5] Ibid., p. 257.
[6] 'The Dark Night of the Soul' in *The Complete Works of Saint John of the Cross*, Vol. I. Translated by E. Allison Peers, London, 1953, p. 330.

There are many difficulties or errors in the first period of Beginners, all clearly set out in the text. Amongst them one easily recognizes the negative transference, including its infantile root, inflation, the will to power, and many other events and processes which modern psychological research has revealed. Perhaps the most striking of all is the emphasis on the pleasure principle as the determining force in the spiritual experience of Beginners.

The First Dark Night is concerned with the purgation of the senses. The Second Dark Night is only reached by a few; it is concerned with purging the spirit. Through both there runs the sense of an inner drama in which all the functions of consciousness are systematically obliterated so that God as a kind of pure essence can operate. They are both full of dangers and pitfalls, but those souls[7] who negotiate them successfully pass on to the union with God, the *unio mystica*, which only comes about completely after death.

The analogy between the process of the Dark Nights and the Mass is close. The whole theme centres round the action of God on the Soul.

God ' . . . binds its interior faculties, and allows it not to cling to the understanding, nor to have delight in the will, nor to reason with the memory.'[8]

Or again:

the ' . . . Divine light of contemplation assails the soul . . . it causes spiritual darkness in it; for not only does it overcome it, but likewise it overwhelms it and darkens the act of its natural intelligence.'[9]

Further, the element of mystery or miracle appears as a fundamental experience. It becomes manifest in the Second Dark Night as the Secret Wisdom which

. . . is so simple, so general and so spiritual that it has not entered into the understanding enwrapped, or clad in any form or image subject to sense, it follows that sense and imagination (as it has not entered through them nor has taken their form and colour) cannot account for it or imagine it, so as to say anything concerning it, although the soul be clearly aware that it is experiencing and partaking of that rare and delectable wisdom.[10]

[7] The soul is identical with the anima inasmuch as she is feminine and mediates between the phenomena of the Godhead and the ego.

[8] Ibid., p. 354, par. 7.   [9] Ibid., p. 382, par. 3.   [10] Ibid., p. 429, par. 3.

These facts, which will be further developed later, make it evident that the Mass and the mystical process are dealing with the same fundamental problem: they are both concerned with the sacrifice to God and the mysterious benefit which accrues from that sacrifice.

But we still have to consider the differences, the most evident of which is that in the ritual of the Mass the soul is not represented, whilst in the mystical process the whole action of God is explicitly directed towards the soul.

The source of the contrast between the ritual and mysticism can surely be found in the difference in circumstances. The ritual takes place in a collective situation within the body of the Holy Mother (the Church). The priest officiates as the spiritual father of his children and invites them to participate in the mystery. The mystical experience, on the other hand, is individual and solitary: the mystic invites the action of God upon the soul as an individual.

These facts can be understood by psychology if we are prepared to look at the phenomena as follows. According to analytical knowledge the following development takes place in the life of the individual. At first the child is united to his parents by the projection of the archetypes on to them. Gradually there develops a personal relationship. At adolescence the initiation of confirmation draws over the archetypal images into the Church, which increases the possibilities of this relationship. Father and mother become Priest and Mother Church, to which is added the spiritual aspect of the mother as the Virgin.

Thus in relation to religion, in relation to the Church, and in relation to God, the ordinary man or woman is kept firmly in the state of a child. This state is of the greatest value for two reasons: (1) because the state of being a 'child' is the necessary prerequisite for entry into the Kingdom of Heaven; (2) because those who are living in the world need to have the archetypal forms of the unconscious held or contained somewhere. Within the Church they are held through regular services and rituals prescribed by her. Thus, though the main activity of the ordinary man is in the world, he never loses touch with the archetypal images, projected into the rituals at the centre of which is the Mass. The Church therefore stands between the ego and the divine mysteries in the same relation as the soul stands between the ego and the mystical communion with God.

St. John's observation makes it quite clear that the soul is not only identical in its functioning but also in its phenomenology with the concept of the soul in analytical psychology, according to which the anima as a soul image is the function of relationship between the ego and the unconscious psyche. She starts to appear at the period in which the separation from the mother begins to take place.

It is an empirical observation that the soul image is formed as projections are withdrawn. The anima is the inner image or vessel in which the previously projected libido is contained. With the aid of this observation we can understand why the soul appears in mysticism as a definite function. It is because the libido projected into the ritual is withdrawn through the mystical introversion.

The symbolism of the Mother comes clearly into our quotations from St. John, which also show the separation or development of the soul image out of its relation to the Mother. The symbolism of the Bride and of the Mother is an established theme in Christianity. It is well known that the Song of Solomon with its erotic symbolism has been extensively interpreted in spiritual terms; the erotic language runs not only through St. John's writings but also through those of other mystics.

This symbolism was worked into Christianity very early in our era. The Christian fathers evidently drew on pagan symbolism extensively and Robert Eisler traces the connexions with Orphism in his book *Orpheus the Fisher*. There the whole symbolism of mother and child is brought into sharp relief: he says, for instance, ' . . . Deceased Christians . . . call themselves on their epitaphs "infants". For according to Tertullian (*Ad Martyres*) they are "children" and even "sucklings" of the Mother Church.'[11] This symbolism was continued into rituals, so that the newly-baptised were actually fed on milk and honey. The Christians were called by Clement of Alexandria *galaktophagoi*, the milk drinkers. 'As the child is vivified,' says the Epistle of Barnabas, vi, 12, 'by honey and milk, so is the faithful by the Word.'[12] Thus the milk is the *logos* ' . . . which flows from the sweet breasts (*apo glykeron maston*) of the mystic bride—the Church.'[13] This symbolism was reinforced, according to Eisler,

[11] Robert Eisler, *Orpheus—The Fisher*. London, 1921, p. 63.
[12] Ibid., p. 64.   [13] Ibid., p. 66.

by reference to the Old Testament, where a root was found in Rachel.

THE METHOD OF ST. JOHN OF THE CROSS

We can now deepen our understanding of St. John's symbolism. The soul is first tempted by God with spiritual milk, which is the *logos*, the word of God.

From the earliest growth of Christianity we find two clear strains of religious development, on the one hand that directed towards organization of the Church, depending for its strength upon the historical correctness of the Gospels, the ritual laying on of hands and the dramatic preservation of the parent images; on the other the individual mystical experiences, which follow in some respects the Gnostic tradition.

These two streams ran to some extent in harmony, but the Church tended to regard mysticism with scepticism on account of the difficulty in assimilating mystical knowledge into the general body of Church doctrine, whilst she wisely elaborated the most careful tests of miraculous events. As a result there was a strong tendency for mystics to drift into the shadow of the Church and become heretical, even though others became eminent ecclesiastics like St. Gregory the Great.

New developments in religious doctrine usually start from individuals. In consequence new discoveries require considerable labour on both sides so that the organization can develop through the vitality of individuals. Those discoveries which could not, for one reason or another, be brought within the scope of the dogma became heretical; those which could be assimilated became part of the Church doctrine and the mystic became canonized as a saint.

St. John spent an enormous amount of time collecting parallels from Biblical sources, partly to clarify his meaning but also, we may assume, to give his knowledge authenticity; almost every experience he describes is supported or amplified by a quotation, more often from the Old Testament than from the New. This work is an important part of his labours, bridging the gap between Church doctrine and individual experience. In the end he has been successful, not however without causing the Church a good deal of trouble!

St. John represents the culmination of a mystical development which faded out gradually after his death. One is almost tempted to call him an analyst, for mysticism had become nearly scientific in his hands. His descriptions are sufficiently detailed to compare with contemporary findings and are usually striking in their objectivity. He describes the symptoms of entry into the Dark Night with exemplary clarity, and he has up to a point that empirical approach which analysis has introduced into psychological research.

He differs from the analytical spirit, however, in important respects; and this is due to the mediaeval outlook in which he was immersed. For him the dogma of the Church was supreme, and we continually find the virtue of obedience brought forward as a cardinal virtue. For this reason the negative transference was very difficult to handle, and we learn that many mystics went astray at this point.[14]

In order to make clear his attitude towards mystical experiences which do not conform to his position, let us look at a 'Judgement given by the Blessed Father upon the Spirituality and Method of Procedure in Prayer of a Nun of our Order.'[15] This communication will at the same time show how the force of authority can be applied and with what aim. St. John lists the following defects in his nun:

First, it appears that she has a great eagerness for possession; Secondly, she has overmuch confidence and few misgivings lest she stray interiorly; Thirdly, she seems anxious to persuade others to believe that her experiences are good and abundant; Fourthly, and most important, there seem to be no signs of humility . . .; Fifthly, the style and language which she here uses do not seem in agreement with the spirituality to which she here lays claim.

In conclusion he says: 'All this that she says about what she said to God, and what God said to her, seems to be nonsense.' His prescription is as follows:

. . . she should be neither ordered nor permitted to write anything about such things as these, nor should her confessor give any appearance of wishing to hear about them, save in order to deprecate them. Let her be tested in the practice of the virtues alone, and especially in self-contempt, humility and obedience. Such acid tests will result in the

[14] Cf. p. 134 below.
[15] *The Complete Works of St. John of the Cross*, trans. E. Allison Peers, Vol. III. London, 1953, pp. 279–80.

purification of her soul, which has received so many favours. But the tests must be severe, for there is no evil spirit that will not undergo some degree of suffering to save his own reputation.

The nun was evidently experiencing an invasion from the unconscious, and it looks as if this had produced an inflation. It would be dealt with in an entirely different spirit if she were in analysis, because analysis has no dogmatic theology out of which it can prescribe such things. We might be doubtful about the value to the individual of her conversations with God, and we are familiar with the fact that there are all sorts of gods within the psyche; we might well consider whether the patient was insane or whether she could stand the invasion; in addition we might decide that the phenomena should not be subjected to analytical reduction; but I do not think any analyst has the right to work it out with the aid of the virtues which St. John cites, because that would lead to repressing the phenomena out of which we should consider healing or wholeness, i.e. individuation, could take place.[16]

The doctrine of wholeness or healing is not altogether absent from St. John when he says that the aim of mysticism is to conform the whole soul in its sensitive and spiritual parts of God. We can see in this at least the idea of the whole, but that cannot work out in reality according to our analytical knowledge. One cannot accomplish it and say at the same time: 'All this that she says about what she said to God, and what God said to her, seems to be nonsense.' To us it seems in some ways an enviable certainty, on the other hand it strikes against what amounts to our whole analytical philosophy of life, which is individual and relative and could only put repression forward as a matter of expediency.

St. John was perfectly in line with the attitude of his period at this point. He lived in the time of the Spanish Inquisition, when the reality of the Devil was so urgent that to listen to him would bring about highly unpleasant consequences, not only spiritual but also material. The whole of Christendom was bent on exterminating the Devil's influence. It was a period of 'burning doubts' which had to be excluded by every means in the power of the Church. That was the spirit of the period, and we have no

[16] Further discussion of this issue is to be found on p. 149 f. below.

right to judge the merit of the mystical work from the standpoint of our own day.

Though St. John had great psychological acumen he did not have the means which we have. Naturally analysts think their position stronger, though not through individual merit, than that of the mystic, and consequently they think it would be regressive to take up his mystical position which is throughout informed, directed, or controlled by dogma. To possess the means of development into a whole is actually better to us than living in a divided state—an essential part of the mediaeval outlook. It is even more religious, according to our ideas, since we should feel obliged to follow up the promptings of the inner voice which had evidently been roused in his nun and which with a keen ear St. John had spotted as the voice, if not of the Devil himself, at least of one of his emissaries.

ASSIMILATING EVIL

We have come upon the difficult problem of assimilating Evil. Owing to our Christian tradition it is a daring and precarious adventure to make any attempt to do so, for so long as any psychic phenomenon is felt to be evil it can today be assimilated, if at all, only with the greatest difficulty. Nevertheless, what we conceive to be evil from subjective prejudice is very often not so in reality. Analysis, therefore, can work at the subjective contents so as to remove the negative valuation of some elements in the psyche. In this way many psychic contents before conceived to be evil can subsequently be assimilated. But by this time they are no longer even thought to be evil.

Over and above these there is real evil, which presents the central problem. For analytical psychology good and evil are indications of relative value; they are a pair of opposites, and though their psychological reality cannot be brought into question the scientific or objective attitude gives them a different significance and brings us into a position different to that usually taken up by religion. The possibility of a solution to this conflict can only come about by reaching a position beyond the opposites; but until the necessary material emerges, the possibility of a solution does not even dawn upon consciousness, and when it does appear it does not do away with good and evil. When the unifying symbol, the self, emerges it is as a natural event, which cannot be brought about by any prescription. It could never become, for instance, a virtue or a duty to assimilate evil! For this reason the nun could not be judged by analysts; she would be treated as an individual with an inner life in her own right.

The individual principle flourishes only to a limited point in Christian mysticism, which is throughout permeated with the absolute idea of the right way and the wrong way; it is in accordance with the mediaeval principle of Hercules at the Crossroads. Christian mysticism has always been suspicious of visions and dreams. St. John depreciates them, and according to him the *scala mystica* leads to the state in which all phenomena of the senses are destroyed and where the Devil has no power. Here he approaches Oriental mysticism with its doctrine of *maya*. The ultimate reality is beyond the illusion of phenomena.

Dreams and visions are, however, meat and drink to the analyst because he seeks to bring the contents of the unconscious into consciousness through the medium of the image, the very thing which mysticism reversed. The whole emphasis of mysticism was upon the unconscious and the phenomena of consciousness were gradually eliminated in a systematic way.

Outside the Church, but overlapping with it, since some of its devotees were actually priests, ran a different stream of individual and more experimental mysticism—alchemy. In contrast to Christian mysticism it was an *opus* the alchemist was working in his laboratory redeeming the *lapis*, the philosopher's stone, from the *materia prima*. The complete abandonment to the unconscious was absent. The alchemist worked in a highly individual and undogmatic way, inventing terminology of his own to describe what he found so that there is an absolute delirium of different terms for the same thing. In addition it may be supposed that the question of heresy made it necessary to adopt a policy of concealment on some topics; add to this the obscure nature of the phenomena with which he dealt, and we can understand the dark cloud which hung over this part of religious history till it gradually cleared as the result of analytical labours. These culminated in Jung's discovery of individuation symbols and led to his comparison of the alchemical process with the individuation process.[17]

[17] Cf. Jung, *Psychology and Alchemy* (Collected Works, Vol. XII). London and New York, 1953, pp. 34 ff.

The alchemists did not know what they were dealing with, but to us there is little doubt about it. The alchemists could not know because they were working with a projection; it was outside themselves, unrelated to them. They eventually began to identify the *lapis* with Christ, and in the end their labours ceased very much at the same period as Christian mysticism began to lose its vitality.

With the death of these two streams of individual religious experience little serious attention appears to have been paid to the inner mystical life. On the contrary, we witness the increasing growth of consciousness which owed its main impetus to the scientific attitude to which dogma is anathema and mysticism the work of the devil. It is at least reasonable to assume that the libido previously flowing into the primordial images became directed into scientific research.

Whether this be the real explanation or not, we know that there is a limit to the activities of consciousness and that we are likely sooner or later to get a reaction from the unconscious. This is clearly what is happening today. The rediscovery of the unconscious psyche was ushered in by philosophy and art to be taken up by psychology; it is also found in the modern revival of mysticism both within and outside the churches.

Medicine only gradually adopted psychological methods to treat mental disorders. At times injudiciously, it has attacked and wrestled with religion in its organized and individual forms. Analytical psychology has especially interested itself in those aspects of religion which can throw light on the phenomena of the unconscious psyche, and has used in a psychological context a terminology which previously had a purely religious meaning. In doing so it has recognized its debt to religion, but has produced a certain confusion, because in using these terms— shadow, anima, the wise man, self—it seems almost to be a new kind of religion. Some people have even mistaken it for such.

ANALYTICAL PSYCHOLOGY

Analytical psychology has two ancestors: on the one hand the method of the natural sciences, on the other hand mysticism and alchemy. It does not disparage its forebears, though it claims to have developed its own roots and its own methods. Consequently it is an original creation. If we like, we could say that it is a new instrument given to us by the grace of God, a new kind of way of understanding God himself. On the other hand a good many prefer to consider it the work of the Devil, failing to realize that, in making them conscious of their relation to the Devil, it increases their possibilities of finding God.

To analytical psychology both these judgements are attitudes of mind, and it consequently cannot be called a religion. As a new child of august parents it can turn back on them and either attack them or contribute towards their further growth. It can say certain things about the working of religion in human beings, and it will think not without reason that its illumination will have some bearing on that metaphysical reality which it does not know. In taking up this attitude it means to express its critical desire to co-operate. It can say, to take up an earlier theme, that what men talk about is not too important; it is a side issue if they argue about the border-line between psychology and religion; but it is really important whether those people who talk have any relationship to their own inner life. If they have not, then they had better not talk and argue so much between themselves, but instead start to pay attention to the voice within them. It can also say that it is very important for some people to be occupied with the unconscious. Experience will make certain that as matters stand only relatively few people will be able to do this, and that the main body of human beings will need to be brought in touch with the unconscious through ritual observances of one sort or another, through religious observance, through art, through the cinema, and perhaps one day through psychiatric clinics.

But the main interest in analysis will certainly go towards developing the personality of the individual and of giving meaning and richness to his or her life. In doing this it must regard religious phenomena as a projection, however certain genuinely religious men and women may be that they are not. It must regard them in this way because it knows that if it does so, a process is set going which actually benefits people and cures them, healing them in a way which nothing else can do.

We have discussed in a short time a good many things which are not very easy to grasp. When any analyst starts to approach religion at all he must lay himself open to such an attack. I once had a patient who was studying to become a clergyman and he showed me the syllabus of his training. It contained things that I had scarcely even heard of, and it contained also a lot of psychology, but his lecturer certainly never understood what psychology was about, if I was to believe what my patient said.

In discussing a religious topic a psychologist is at a disadvantage; he risks, through his lack of training in the host of subjects which cling round the sophisticated aspects of religion, the reproach of being elementary, amateurish, or even grossly wrong. In my opinion at least he should not be deterred by this reproach. His actual naïveté may well make it possible for him to discover something new where others have failed. On the other hand he has the definite advantage that in handling people he is simply forced to handle religious experiences, which he must take quite seriously. In these cases, it is little use appealing to traditional theology, which the patient has usually rejected out of hand, and so he has to turn in another direction for aid. That aid is provided by analytical psychology, with the help of which the experience can be related to the life of the individual. Without this application to actual life the experience does not come into consciousness but remains projected into the outer world.

That is the reality I should like to emphasize. The contribution of analytical psychology to religion is this: it brings religious experience home to the individual in a way which nothing else can do; it brings it home as a psychological fact. This is surely a most important event. Moreover, in bringing home the possibility of becoming a whole or real individual we are following, in however humble and insignificant a way, what religion has always termed the will of God.

IX

'THE DARK NIGHT OF THE SOUL'[1]

IN 1944 I read *The Dark Night of the Soul*[2] for the first time
and was immediately struck by the similarities it records
with analytic phenomena. The two sets of experience are
also remarkable for their differences, which is only to be expected,
for its author, St. John, lived in Spain four centuries ago. He was
born in 1542 and died in 1591, in a mental climate very different
from that of today. To us it may be clear that the position of the
Catholic Church was somewhat uncertain because at this period
the Inquisition was at its height and St. John himself felt its
heavy hand, but to St. John there can have been no doubt. He
became a mystic as a consequence of a vision and was utterly
dedicated to the rigours of a mystical life whose sole aim was to
draw nearer and nearer to the divine mystery of union with God.

The numerous differences need not, however, lead to the
under-estimation of similarities. The differences are naturally of
great interest, most of all perhaps to the historian, because he will
be drawn to consider the changes in consciousness that take place
over the years. To the analytical psychologist, however, the un-
changing objective archetypal forms can occupy the main centre
of attention. These express themselves over and over again in
each age, meeting the prevailing conscious attitude of the period
which gives rise to variations behind which he seeks to penetrate. If the aim is to get behind the conscious forms, similarities

[1] Originally published as 'The Analytical Approach to Mysticism',
Revue suisse de Psychologie et de Psychologie appliquée, Vol. IV, Nos. 3–4.
The present version has been revised.

[2] There are many who do not like psychologists laying their profane
hands on mystical works. I can only hope that this dislike will not make
them pass over the contributions of analysts like myself, whose study of
religious texts, however haphazard it may be and however inadequate in
numerous respects, has given them a respect for the great religions and
for their exponents which they could not otherwise have felt.

will be the first consideration. Once these are established, they will again throw the differences into relief.

This comparative method will be used here in order to study the relation of analytical psychology to the mystic. Analytical psychology has often been called mystical, rather as a term of abuse than anything else, but the comparison keeps recurring, and lately has been given more authoritative expression by Dr. Quispel, who arraigns Jung amongst the Gnostics.

Before this study of St. John's great writings I must confess to having felt some concern at being reproached for mysticism. Now, as the result of this study I should have no objection to being called a mystic if it were true. This essay will not solve the general problem of whether analytical psychology is mystical but it will, I hope, contribute towards putting the issue upon a more dignified basis than heretofore.

The Dark Night of the Soul must be of particular interest to a practising analyst because it records not only the individual experiences of St. John but also those of other mystics for whom he had acted as confessor and whom he was able to direct along the exacting path of mystical revelation because of his own experiences.

St. John's mysticism had become almost technical. Behind it lay centuries of experience and study, but the emphasis undoubtedly lay most on experience as the necessary prerequisite for the initiation of others. Here at the outset is an analogy with analytical psychology.

The Dark Night of the Soul is a description of the soul's journey in search of God. This journey is an introverted process which involves as a fundamental tenet renunciation of the world, the flesh, and the devil, from which the soul is protected by the three virtues of faith, hope, and charity. Starting on a human plane, it gradually becomes more and more remote from earthly life till the climax is reached with the ascent of the *scala mystica* and the final union with God—the *unio mystica*—after the death of the body. Though the final union takes place only after death, yet the soul is able, in this world, to come into an intimate relation with God, through which relation many sublime results are said to accrue.

The main bulk of the book is made up of a commentary on the 'Stanzas of the Soul', a poem whose erotic language is understood by St. John throughout in a spiritual sense. The love is the divine love of God to which the soul has dedicated herself, and the 'Stanzas of the Soul' are composed by a soul that

is now in the state of perfection, which is the union of love with God, having already passed through severe trials and straits, by means of spiritual exercise in the narrow way of eternal life whereof Our Saviour speaks in the Gospel, along which way the soul ordinarily passes in order to reach this high and happy union with God.[3]

STANZAS OF THE SOUL

1. On a dark night, Kindled in love with yearnings—oh, happy chance!—
   I went forth without being observed, My house being now at rest.

2. In darkness and secure, By the secret ladder, disguised—oh, happy chance!—
   In darkness and in concealment, My house being now at rest.

3. In the happy night, In secret, when none saw me,
   Nor I beheld aught, Without light or guide, save that which burned in my heart.

4. This light guided me More surely than the light of noonday
   To the place where he (well I knew who!) was awaiting me—
   A place where none appeared.

5. Oh, night that guided me, Oh, night more lovely than the dawn,
   Oh, night that joined Beloved with lover, Lover transformed in the Beloved!

6. Upon my flowery breast, Kept wholly for himself alone,
   There he stayed sleeping, and I caressed him, And the fanning of the cedars made a breeze.

7. The breeze blew from the turret As I parted his locks;
   With his gentle hand he wounded my neck And caused all my senses to be suspended.

8. I remained, lost in oblivion; My face I reclined on the Beloved.
   All ceased and I abandoned myself, Leaving my cares forgotten among the lilies.

[3] *Complete Works of Saint John of the Cross*, translated by E. Allison Peers. London, 1953, Vol. I, p. 326.

The commentary, with which we shall deal later in more detail, applies only to the first two stanzas; these alone are concerned with the Dark Night. The last six stanzas depict the benefits which come to the soul as the result of the Dark Night, which is therefore a true *transitus*. The Dark Night will be adequately amplified later, but for the sake of convenience we may now consider one or two features of the poem which do not need more extensive elaboration. The house refers to the faculties of the soul, which have to be dealt with by 'purgation' before she is able to realize the benefits which result from the first dark experiences of God. It will be noted at this juncture that the house is stated to be *now* at rest; it had not been, and the phrase suggests that it might not be again.

The secret ladder refers to the *scala mystica*; it is secret because of its dark, secret, or unfathomable nature. The disguise strikes one as peculiar, but it has a definite connotation. It indicates the necessity for protection against the three enemies of the soul: the world, the flesh, and the devil, whose repeated onslaughts St. John describes in some detail.

Thus the livery which it wears is of three chief colours—white, green and purple—denoting the three theological virtues, faith, hope and charity. By these the soul will not only gain the grace and goodwill of its Beloved, but it will travel in security and complete protection from its three enemies.[4]

Following 'Stanzas of the Soul' is the commentary, and we shall now examine some of the passages of the text which can be understood in the light of analytical psychology. We shall not attempt to embrace the whole of the mystical experience, but shall simply seek to study something of the relation of analysis to mysticism, by the comparative method.

There are three phases in the mystical experience, all initiated by the action of God on the soul. Throughout the whole process God is the prime mover and the soul a passive agent; it is God that causes the purgation. The first phase is preparatory and those in this period are called beginners; the next phase is concerned with the first Dark Night, in which the senses of the soul are thoroughly purged; the second and last Dark Night purges the soul of all its spiritual activity so that the pure light of God's

---

[4] Ibid., p. 442, par. 3.

spiritual love may guide the soul up the ten steps of the *scala mystica*, through the stages of more and more burning and lofty love of God, to the final union, in which the whole soul 'conforms' itself to God. Those in the last two phases are termed progressive in contrast to the beginners. Between each two stages there is a period of spiritual quiescence of longer or shorter duration, and as we progress, fewer and fewer souls succeed in passing the severe tests to which they are subjected.

St. John says that the first stirrings of the spirit derive from God who tempts the soul to taste of spiritual pleasures by offering his breast of tender love (the loving mother which is like the grace of God):

> It must be known, then, that the soul, after it has been definitely converted to the service of God, is, as a rule, spiritually nurtured and caressed by God, even as is the tender child by its loving mother, who warms it with the heat of her bosom and nurtures it with sweet milk and soft and pleasant food, and carries it and caresses it in her arms.[5]

This pleasure provides the first source of error, for the delight it produces tends to result in spiritual intoxication so that many souls imagine they have got much further than is really the case, in short, they think that they know all there is to be known; nowadays we call this inflation. Thus early do we find a clear-cut description of a familiar event in the process of analysis. It is this inflation which causes difficulties. The beginners will not submit to their spiritual advisers, upon whom they project their infantile shadow ' . . . they either change or vary or add to that which is commanded them, as any obedience in this respect is so bitter to them.'[6] With penetrating clarity St. John grasps the nature of this difficulty. In a similar way to Freud, he grasps the infantile aspect of the transference: '. . . they become as peevish as children and go about in great displeasure, thinking that they are not serving God when they are not allowed to do that which they would.'[7] And again: 'They are, in fact, as we have said, like children who are not influenced, neither act by reason, but from pleasure.'[8]

The first section of the book, dealing with problems of beginners, is an exceedingly human document, and in this respect it

[5] Ibid., p. 330, par. 2.   [6] Ibid., p. 334, par. 2.
[7] Ibid., pp. 344-5, par. 2.   [8] Ibid., p. 346, par. 6 (literal translation).

contrasts with the later part, which becomes more and more remote from human experience, more and more inhuman and incomprehensible. It contains a description of all the ways in which beginners depart from the prescribed way. St. John calls these departures imperfections, and his point of view is comparable to that of analysis, which tries to view the patients' difficulties in terms of their own inner conflicts and avoids moral censure. The imperfections are as follows: spiritual pride, avarice, voluptuousness, anger, gluttony, envy, and sluggishness. St. John goes into them at some length. As one reads it becomes clear that in substance it is concerned with how to handle the pleasure that spiritual exercises bring with them. In this respect the descriptions are not unlike psycho-analysis, which was founded on the pleasure principle, though it identified pleasure with psycho-sexual gratification alone.

St. John describes how God starts to withdraw the breast:

> . . . as the child grows bigger, the mother gradually ceases caressing it, and, hiding her tender love, puts bitter aloes upon her sweet breast, sets down the child from her arms and makes it walk upon its feet, so that it may lose the habits of a child and betake itself to more important and substantial occupations.[9]

Thus we meet at once an event made familiar to us as 'separation anxiety'.

Modern knowledge, particularly Freud's work, has made many analysts sceptical of spiritual experience, seeing in it mere sexual sublimation. The 'Stanzas of the Soul' is indeed highly suggestive in this respect so that we eagerly look to see what St. John has to say on the subject.

In St. John's experience, the soul is divided into two parts, a spiritual part and a sensual or sensitive part. It is the sensitive part from which apparently psycho-sexual manifestations arise. These are most insistent and obstinate in their activity, and there can be little doubt that sexual feelings get into the most sacred rites:

> For it often comes to pass that, in their very spiritual exercises, when they are powerless to prevent it, there arise and assert themselves in the sensual part of the soul impure acts and motions, and sometimes this happens even when the spirit is deep in prayer, or taking part in the

[9] Ibid., p. 330, par. 2.

Sacrament of Penance or in the Eucharist. These things are not, as I say, in their power; they proceed from one of three causes.

The first cause from which they often proceed is the pleasure which human nature takes in spiritual things. For when the spirit and the sense are pleased, every part of a man is moved by that pleasure to delight according to its proportion and nature. For then the spirit, which is the higher part, is moved to pleasure and delight in God; and the sensual nature, which is the lower part, is moved to pleasure and delight of the senses, because it cannot possess and lay hold upon aught else, and it therefore lays hold upon that which comes nearest to itself, which is the impure and sensual. Thus it comes to pass that the soul is in deep prayer with God according to the spirit, and, on the other hand, according to sense it is passively conscious, not without great displeasure, of rebellions and motions and acts of the senses, which often happens in Communion, for when the soul receives joy and comfort in this act of love, because this Lord bestows it (since it is to that end that He gives Himself), the sensual nature takes that which is its own likewise, as we have said, after its manner.[10]

It would be inaccurate to think that St. John means sexuality in its biological sense, though it is scarcely conceivable that sexual impulses do not manifest themselves since 'every part of man is moved'; he rather refers to an inner or spiritual event as the prime mover. The imperfections of mysticism are not the ordinary seven deadly sins of Christian dogma, which are supposed to have been already overcome; so what is the nature of the unclean impulses? He does not say openly, but if we turn to St. Augustine's *Confessions* we can, I think, see more clearly the nature of the process to which St. John refers.

St. Augustine's conversion freed him from the lusts of the flesh. A central conflict in his early life was concerned with actual sexual relations: he was unable to give up his mistress who stood in the way of his conversion to Christianity. But he did not, by separating from her, finally resolve the conflict. St. Augustine says:

Assuredly You command that I contain myself from the *lust of the flesh, the lust of the eyes, and the pride of life*. You commanded me also to abstain from fornication, and in the matter of marriage You advised me a better course though you allowed me a less good. And since You gave me the power, it was so done, even before I became a dispenser of Your Sacrament. Yet there still live in my memory the images of those things,

[10] Ibid., pp. 338–9, par. 2.

of which I have already spoken much, which my long habit had fixed there. When I awake they beset me though with no great power, but in sleep not only seeming pleasant, but even to the point of consent and the likeness of the act itself. The illusion of that image is of such avail in my soul and in my flesh, that mere visions persuade me in sleep as the realities could not persuade me when I am awake.[11]

I think these examples make it sufficiently clear that mysticism approaches the same sphere as Freud but, whereas mystics approach it in a moral way and are probably concerned, as we shall see, to repress it, Freud refrains from this attitude; indeed he regards sex as the most vital function of the human organism and so is utterly opposed to mysticism.

If, however, we look more closely into Freud's theories we shall discover quasi-mystical ideas of death and eternity. In mysticism death is an aim because without the departure of the soul from its physical body there could be no final union of the soul with God in eternal love. It is true that a great deal of the soul's path to God could be accomplished in this life, St. John specifically states, for instance, that the second Dark Night is identical with purgatory, but the final *unio mystica* needs the death of the body for its accomplishment.

Let us turn to Freud's speculative notions about life and death. He says that there are two instincts, the sex instinct, which he later terms Eros, and the death instinct, which he calls Thanatos; Eros is, in a sense, eternal because it perpetuates itself. The sexual cells are indeed the only ones which survive the death of the body. On the contrary, the death instincts arise out of the body, whose aim is consequently to die; it is Eros in its narcissistic form which therefore preserves life at all. Thus, we have in Freud a notion which is certainly analogous to the mystical one, and both recognize death as an aim, so that we may well be led to assume that each is dealing with the same essential element or archetype. It is known, however, that Freud criticized the validity of religious experience and, in doing so, expressed a view which belongs to our time: it has found political expression in Russia, whilst it is widely held by individuals, either implicitly or explicity, all over the world, who know little or nothing of psychoanalysis or, for that matter, of mysticism.

This view is not, however, established even in the psycho-

[11] *Confessions of St. Augustine*, trans. F. J. Sheed. London, 1944, p. 190.

logical sphere. On the contrary, Jung has shown, to my mind convincingly, that the spiritual principle, the spiritual soul of St. John, cannot be destroyed, but merely changes its form and mode of expression under the criticism which has been directed towards it. We have tried to indicate the kind of change which can occur as a result of the impact of Freud's work; if this be taken in conjunction with Jung's, the spiritual experience now appears as an essential part of the integrating process of individuation with which we find strong analogies. The whole development is similar; there is the separation from infantile dominants which St. John understands in terms of separation from God's breast, the resolution of the transference in its infantile aspects, but most striking of all is the experience of the soul which, if stripped of its theological interpretation, is simply identical with Jung's description of the *anima*. The soul in both cases is purely objective, a female 'person'. We are not concerned in the Dark Night with what happens to a living man, but to the soul which is conceived of as a separate entity. She is quite separate from the ego, an autonomous being whose experiences can be described in an objective way. Moreover, just as Jung says the soul is the organ of inner perception, so in the Dark Night she is subject to visions, dreams and, as we have seen, sensual and instinctive 'motions', whilst she alone experiences God.

Once over the stage of the 'beginners' the soul enters the Dark Night in all its intensity. The Dark Night is also called the purgative night and is divided into two parts:

. . . the one night or purgation will be sensual, wherein the soul is purged according to sense, which is subdued to the spirit; and the other is a night or purgation which is spiritual, wherein the soul is purged and stripped according to the spirit, and subdued and made ready for the union of love with God.[12]

By the senses St. John does not mean sensuality, but what one may call object love, that is to say, material objects or objects of the imagination, visions and dreams. In other words, all the functions of relation to the outer world, and all but one of the images, namely God as light, from the unconscious, are systematically destroyed or purged by the divine action. It is for this reason that the experience is called the Dark Night of the soul, for

[12] *The Complete Works of Saint John of the Cross*, Vol. I, p. 349, par. 1.

. . . when this Divine light of contemplation assails the soul which is not yet wholly enlightened, it causes spiritual darkness in it; for not only does it overcome it, but likewise it overwhelms it and darkens the act of its natural intelligence.[13]

For one whose aim is to treat the psyche in as scientific a way as possible it is particularly pleasant to find the features of entry into the Dark Night described clearly and systematically. The soul, we discover, finds no pleasure in anything, the attention becomes fixed on God, a sense of dryness and displeasure, a feeling of the soul that she does not serve God. We learn that the soul sinks into a state of silence and solitude, she does nothing but allows herself '. . . to be led by God, to receive and to listen with loving interior attentiveness . . .'[14] and '. . . if it desires to work with its faculties, it hinders the work which God is doing in it rather than aids it.'[15]

In the place of mental activity, in the place of prayer, thought, argument and meditation arises the process of contemplation, which consists in leaving

. . . the soul free and disencumbered and at rest from all knowledge and thought, troubling not themselves, in that state, about what they shall think or meditate upon, but contenting themselves with merely a peaceful and loving attentiveness toward God, and in being without anxiety, without the ability and without the desire to have experience of Him or to perceive Him. For all these yearnings disquiet and distract the soul from the peaceful quiet and sweet ease of contemplation which is here granted to it.[16]

Then God will work upon the soul: 'He binds its interior faculties, and allows it not to cling to the understanding, nor to have delight in the will, nor to reason with the memory.'[17]

This description reminds us of active imagination, but contrasts with it in essential respects, for whereas analytical psychology values consciousness, St. John's mysticism leads him to the elimination of all conscious functions. God, as the dynamic force of the whole experience, demands this. Thus the process involves total renunciation of the ego to the unconscious, a symbolic death which prepares the soul for its final liberation from

[13] Ibid., p. 382, par. 3.   [14] Ibid., p. 354, fn. 1.
[15] Ibid., p. 354, par. 7.   [16] Ibid., pp. 357–8, par. 4.
[17] Ibid., p. 354, par. 7.

the body whose real death will release her for the sublime and eternal union with God in the hereafter. What could be further from the studies of analytical psychology, whose aim is self-realization as a process of individuation?

Quite apart from its use of the images, which a large section of mystics depreciate, amongst whom we must number St. John, analysis is usually conceived as a descent into the depths which would seem to be totally different from the Christian aim of rising to ever higher spiritual achievements. The mythological parallel to this process of descent is termed the Night Journey on the Sea, about which a large collection of myths has been made by Frobenius. But such is the paradoxical nature of the psyche that what is higher is united with what is lower; therefore the 'Night Journey' and the 'Dark Night' become united in St. John's study: the Dark Night is itself described as a descent into Hell. When the soul is stripped of the Old Adam, he says:

The Divine assails the soul in order to renew it and thus to make it Divine; and, stripping it of the habitual affections and attachments of the old man, to which it is very closely united, knit together and conformed, destroys and consumes its spiritual substance, and absorbs it in deep and profound darkness. As a result of this, the soul feels itself to be perishing and melting away, in the presence and sight of its miseries, in a cruel spiritual death, even as if it had been swallowed by a beast and felt itself being devoured in the darkness of its belly, suffering such anguish as was endured by Jonah in the belly of that beast of the sea. For in this sepulchre of dark death it must needs abide until the spiritual resurrection which it hopes for.[18]

We here hit upon a further interesting feature of St. John's method, to which we cannot refrain from referring in brief; this is his use of biblical material to amplify the context. Over and over again he uses the myth to assist in revealing what is meant. In the passage quoted above we find him using the myth of Jonah to show what the experience is like. In doing so he does not usually use the myth as an analogy, but rather as an illustration. He says in many different ways: this is the experience which Jonah, Job, etc., actually underwent, and thus he is one of those who grasped the essential nature of the Biblical texts. They are revelations of a mystical, or as we should say today, of a psychological nature, and, as such, are true.

[18] Ibid., pp. 384–5, par. 1.

It appears to me that this is a striking anticipation of Jung's concept of the objective psyche and the collective unconscious, whilst St. John's method is to be compared with that used by Jung in his researches and which he called amplification.

We have referred earlier to the line of the poem 'My house being now at rest'. The 'house at rest' sounds suspicious, for we are familiar with sleep as a symptom of repression, while the constant efforts to exclude the Devil and his activity, together with the renunciation in which a mystic of this school becomes involved, go far to support the idea. On general grounds it is likely that repression must occur, but can we not find internal evidence of this in the text?

Those who are especially gifted in spiritual matters, we learn, are filled with the most horrible temptations. '. . . the angel of Satan presents himself—namely, the spirit of fornication—that he may buffet their senses with abominable and violent temptations . . .',[19] all of which are sent to harden the soul. 'For, if the soul be not tempted, proved and exercised with trials and temptations, it cannot quicken its senses for Wisdom'.[20] Further we learn that after the First Dark Night there is a period of quiescence and then, at the onset of the Second or Spiritual Purgation, the phenomena of the sensitive soul return '. . . since the one is never truly purged without the other . . .'.[21] This goes far towards supporting the idea that repression takes an important part in the whole experience, since this sentence cannot fail to make any analyst think of the return of the repressed contents. If we require further evidence we learn that those who are not sufficiently spiritual suffer '. . . raptures and trances and dislocations of the bones . . .',[22] and finally the whole notion of purgation by God and the elimination of the sensual parts seems to give final evidence of it.[23]

The result of the activity of God upon the soul in the Dark Night is intense suffering, the description of which fills much of the book: 'The first purgation or night is bitter and terrible to sense, as we shall now show. The second bears no comparison with it, for it is horrible and awful to the spirit . . .'.[24] The result

[19] Ibid., p. 372, par. 1.   [20] Ibid., p. 372, par. 4.
[21] Ibid., p. 378, par. 1.   [22] Ibid., p. 375, par. 2.
[23] For further discussion of repression as part of the structure of Christianity, cf. p. 149 below.   [24] Ibid., pp. 349–50, par. 2.

is 'illuminating' beyond description—it is the Secret Wisdom, which

. . . is so simple, so general and so spiritual that it has not entered into the understanding enwrapped or cloaked in any form or image subject to sense, it follows that sense and imagination (as it has not entered through them nor has taken their form and colour) cannot account for it or imagine it, so as to say anything concerning it, although the soul be clearly aware that it is experiencing and partaking of that rare and delectable wisdom.[25]

In our efforts to construct a scientific psychology we cannot follow the mystic in his course at this point. The realization of a wisdom which cannot be grasped, which completely baffles any description and so any scientific approach, at once destroys the concept that events can be expressed and understood and, in a measure, controlled; nor can he be followed in his apparent conviction that the final *unio mystica* between the soul and her lover, God, occurs only after death. St. John must refer, not to empirical fact, but to an act of faith in the Church dogma which is fundamental to the whole basis of his mysticism. Without it, the mutilation of the flesh, the scourgings, the struggle with the devil, the separation from the material world as far as is actually possible, would be meaningless. Any suggestion that the basis is wrong would be stillborn by being stigmatized as the work of the Devil. The Secret Wisdom is irrational, likewise the Christian dogma.

We have, however, learnt in psychology out of painful experience that irrational forces or archetypes can far outstrip in effectiveness the power of reason, so that we are bound to treat them with proper respect. Let us, therefore, approach the matter in a different way by considering the common factor in the dogma and the Secret Wisdom. Both contain a sense of overpowering mystery.

To a scientist, mystery is a challenge, he wishes to clear it up, to make it evident, and this is surely the basis of scientific objection to and revulsion from mysticism, which delights in sublime mystery for its own sake because it partakes of the essential nature of God. Yet what is it that produces the discoveries of science, what is it that keeps the research worker at his research, if it is not the activity of the sense of mystery? In

[25] Ibid., p. 429, par. 3.

this connection Russell has noted the religious quality about science; he says:

Until quite recently men of science have felt themselves the high-priests of a noble cult, namely, the cult of truth; not truth as the religious sects understand it, i.e. as the battle-ground of a collection of dogmatists, but truth as a quest, a vision faintly appearing and again vanishing, a hoped-for sun to meet the Heraclitean fire in the soul. It is because science was so conceived that men of science were willing to suffer privations and persecutions, and to be execrated as enemies of established creeds.[26]

But, nevertheless, the scientific and religious attitudes to mystery are opposed. Science and dogmatic faith are inevitably opposed. Change, discovery, and the new development of knowledge are all part and parcel of science. It has proof of its value every day inasmuch as there is a continual spate of new discoveries, whilst religions, though they change and develop, tend to be fundamentally conservative.

We have tried to show how the phenomena of mysticism can be grasped by psychology. Let us therefore suppose a scientist were confronted with the Secret Wisdom or with the *unio mystica*. He would say that we here meet a problem which is insoluble because we look at it in the wrong way; he would then retrace his steps and start from the assumptions. If he does this he is bound to criticize the whole basis of Christian faith in the dogma. If he takes the dogma of the historical Jesus, which stands at the core of Christianity, he will find that the objective facts which prove it are scanty, whilst if he has psychological inclinations he will note substantial motives for establishing Christ as an historical figure. On the one hand it underlines Christ's objectivity, which is of great psychological value because it prevents identification of the individual ego with his unconscious Christianity, whilst on the other hand it can prevent immediate religious experience unless it is fed to him by the Church in its observances. He will note that, besides its value to the individual, it is decidedly to the advantage of the Church to do this and to keep the power in its own hands. On this account the early Fathers, who were building the Church, would be likely, though quite unconsciously, to accept the evidence which cohered rather than that which did not.

[26] Bertrand Russell, *The Scientific Outlook*. London, 1931, pp. 102–3.

These are some of the doubts which must assail the scientific man who brings his intelligence to bear upon the dogma. Science could only dare to take the historical Jesus as a possibility, and would never found its very existence, as the Church itself did, upon such a hypothesis. But if this criticism were accepted, Christian mysticism would cease to exist in its mediaeval form and its interpretation would be shaken to its roots. It is to those who take the scientific spirit seriously that psychology is able to bring at least some measure of understanding to bear upon religious doubts of this sort.

Though it is sometimes considered possible I need not deny here that the whole of religion is ever likely to be reduced to psychology. Indeed, as psychologists we could not do better than adopt some Christian humility and say that the psyche is a comparatively untrodden field; it is a realm which is so new, so unknown, so full of mystery that it terrifies the life out of the majority of humanity, who simply think that the discovery of the unconscious mind is a misconception of facts or mere nonsense. Yet any analyst knows that the unconscious can be absolutely fatal to individual lives, can bring ruin and despair to those who ignore its activity. No practising analyst would relinquish the facts of his everyday experience; the existence of unconscious mental processes is one of them.

This knowledge helps us to give up dogma without abandoning the sense of mystery which draws the scientist on to new discovery. The sense of mystery is itself a psychological fact which we do not know how to formulate unless we realize that nobody has ever succeeded in exhausting the contents of the unconscious, which remains an essential but mysterious part of our nature. From this position we can begin to go further in expressing the scientific and the religious content of our natures. We are led, however, to psychological relativity since nobody can ever get outside his own experience, so that any statement I or anybody else may make is in the nature of a confession.

This digression has led us seemingly a long way from St. John. Let us return to him and see where our psychological approach leads us. It impels us to relate his experience to his own nature, and to ask with particular care just what kind of person St. John was, so as to relate the processes through which he went to his personality. It appears that his experience was personally fruitful; St. Teresa had a good opinion of him; she picked him out from amongst the others as a real Saint, a striking personality, and there appears to be a general agreement about his goodness. He was of a retiring disposition, he never willingly became involved in political or other public controversy, but preferred to give himself up to solitude and the contemplation of the soul's journey to God. He was a scholar, wrote poetry and certainly interesting prose, liked music, he was a reasonably good administrator. He was, in short, an introvert, probably with a good brain, thinking, and with a feeling life which is embodied in his inner experience of Divine Love, and appearing in his poetry and music.

The introverted man is not just a recluse, nor is he necessarily inferior in his relations to other human beings, but he never approaches others with open arms and he is liable to get caught in the activities of those more expert in extraversion. In this respect, St. John's life is quite characteristic. He was, on one occasion, involved quite against his will in a controversy between the Discalced Order, which had been started by St. Teresa, and the more orthodox Friars of the Mitigated Rule; he was simply seized illegally by the latter and put in prison, where he was incarcerated for eight and a half months before he escaped. It was while in prison that he is said to have written much of his best mystical books and poetry.

If an introvert becomes active in the world he has to proceed by applying his own discoveries, which come out of his introversion, to the world, and this, it would seem, is what St. John did. He went about the country preaching, and founding monasteries from the groups of persons whom he attracted to himself by the force of his personality. Later on he achieved an administrative position, but when his convictions were at stake, he at once challenged his more powerful and astute adversary; he was forced to retire. At this time he wrote to Sister Anne of Jesus in a way so characteristic of the introvert that I cannot refrain from quoting at least a fragment of this letter:

. . . it is (he says) very advantageous for me, since, now that I am free and no longer have charge of souls, I can, by Divine favour, if I so desire, enjoy peace, solitude and the delectable fruit of forgetfulness of self and of all things.[27]

[27] *The Complete Works of Saint John of the Cross*, ed. cit., Vol. III, p. 270.

Life in the world was never his métier, and he preferred and felt more at home in the mystical inner world. If we need further information to confirm our view of his introverted nature, we may point to the peculiar fascination and power which objects are liable to have over him. We know that the unconscious compensates the conscious attitude by drawing the individual towards the object, albeit by means of a magical fascination. As St. John's conscious aim is the direct experience of God as spirit, all material objects, amongst which we must include the body, will therefore tend to exert a compulsive quasi-magical tie. That is the personal reason why he denied all creature comforts, why he was amongst those who castigated and mortified the flesh with such vigour, why he could accept the Discalced Order which specialized in austerities, why he chose at one time to live in a tumbledown house with only two objects of importance, skulls and a Cross, as furniture. If he did not do all this he would too easily fall a prey to the object. Thus in *The Dark Night of the Soul* he inveighs against the fascination of objects and describes how he had to remove a wooden cross from 'a person' because he became so much attached to it that it got in the way of his spiritual development. We are further told how he had to destroy St. Teresa's letters, and he must have done this for the same reason.

If we return again to the 'Stanzas of the Soul' we find it couched in terms of erotic feeling. We have an interesting parallel to this—the *Song of Solomon*—which was written as a love poem but was subsequently interpreted by the Jewish and Christian Fathers in symbolical or spiritual terms. This provides, I think, a clue to the problem which I referred to earlier. In mediaeval mysticism we find spiritual problems expressed in erotic language, whilst Freud's theory of instinct leads him towards a mystical concept. Whichever road is taken you necessarily come to the same mystery. There is no way of avoiding the fundamental but irrational facts of instinct on the one hand and spirit on the other.

St. John's way is to renounce the instinct gratifications. This is greatly helped by the support of the dogma which reinforces the inner psychical renunciation and supports the effort at exterminating or repressing the instinct by pointing to the power of the Devil in this sphere. But, inasmuch as this renunciation cannot ever be satisfying during this life, the only dogma which can prove effective is one which asserts the evidence of another world of spiritual bliss which is real and accessible to the human soul after the body has been destroyed, i.e. after death. In other words, without dogma we cannot arrive at St. John's form of mystical development.

The nearest analogy to the *unio mystica* in analytical psychology is the conjunction,[28] i.e. union of the unconscious with the conscious, from which the *self* emerges. The self includes within it spirit and instinct (the mythological earth) which it has become possible to accept intellectually through the development of biological science; Freud drove home the lessons of biology by developing a technique for bringing man into direct contact with his instincts, and in doing so extracted them from the realm of demonology. It follows that if the Devil no longer has power in this region, there are fewer theological grounds for rejecting them. Consequently we cannot today expect the same development from introversion as that which prevailed in the Middle Ages.

The concept of mental health assumes that man can be a whole, comprising spirit and instinct. The concept does not, however, make it come about, since it is in reality an enormously difficult achievement which has to be experienced to be effective. This element of experience is contained in mysticism to a high degree, and the union of the soul, in both her aspects, is the same aim as that found in individuation. That the final mystical solution is mysterious and only occurs after death puts it outside the psychological as well as the human realms.

In so far as it can be understood psychologically, it appears that the development in *The Dark Night of the Soul* is one-sided. There is a secret because there really is something concealed, and so mystery is inevitable and desirable. The concealed element must be the other side, i.e. the Devil. Psychological research has led us to conclude that both sides are contained in the

[28] Cf. Jung, 'The Psychology of the Transference', *The Practice of Psychotherapy* (Collected Works, Vol. XVI). London and New York, 1954. It needs to be pointed out that the *unio mystica* is conceived and darkly experienced as a transcendental reality. The transcendental reality of God cannot be grasped by psychological means or techniques, consequently it would not be justifiable to identify the *unio mystica* with the conjunction.

unconscious; there the pairs of opposites lie together: spirit and instinct, God and Devil. But the dogma asserts that God is not united with the Devil and so the Devil must have escaped.

From time immemorial man has suffered from certain awe-inspiring experiences which he has called God, and till recently they have always been outside or at least separate from his own nature.

The gods at first lived in superhuman power and beauty on the top of snow-clad mountains or in the darkness of caves, woods, and seas. Later on they drew together into one god, and then that god became man. But in our day even the God-man seems to have descended from his throne and to be dissolving himself in the common man. That is probably why his seat is empty.

It is Jung's achievement to have grasped this, and analytical psychology is faced with the problem of conforming the soul to God, just as St. John attempted it in a theological and mystical way; the techniques alter and so does the experience, only the archetypes of the unconscious do not change.

If analysts insist on paying attention to mystical matters using psychological techniques, in contrast to those of theology, it is because by doing so they get a much better idea of man's nature. Instead of pointing to the groves, the trees, the mountains, the sky or the heavens as the source of divine power, or removing it out of reach of experience through metaphysical argument, attention is directed to ourselves and, in doing so, we limit ourselves to what really can be known. In this way we can handle the material so that it is brought into closer relation with our actual lives, so as to enrich our understanding and our natures as a whole.

[29] 'Psychology and Religion' in *Psychology and Religion: West and East* (Collected Works, Vol. XI). London and New York, 1958, p. 84.

X

REPRESSION IN CHRISTIAN PRACTICES

FATHER OSWALD SUMNER wrote 'St. John of the Cross and Modern Psychology'[1] partly in reply to my essay 'Analytical Experience and Religion'[2] because he felt that 'certain clarifications . . . are called for if we are to do full justice to the person and teachings of St. John' (p. 4). In this essay I shall continue the dialogue, because it will help to show up some of the difficulties in relating analytical psychology to Roman Catholic theology, and at the same time give me an opportunity to amplify some of my earlier statements which were too compressed.

The core of Father Sumner's argument is given in the following quotations: 'Right from the start we must remember that St. John of the Cross begins his treatise at the point where the psychologist considers that the integration of the personality, or the process of individuation, has been reached' (p. 8), and later: 'St. John is aiming at precisely the highest known form of wholeness, infinitely surpassing, as I have pointed out, the wholeness which is reached at a stage of individuation possible to those who are not called to a spiritual life' (p. 29). He means that St. John is concerned with the grace of God of which the divine ray is a manifestation: 'For we have a theological principle that grace builds on nature—and if nature is in a mess then grace waits, as a rule, for nature to be put in order before acting in a strong and paramount manner' (p. 11).

He supports his thesis by detailing the conditions for the mystical life,[3] which differ from those known to any analyst in being

---

[1] *Guild Lecture, No. 57*, Guild of Pastoral Psychology Pamphlet, December 1948.

[2] *Guild Lecture No. 46*, March 1947.   [3] Sumner, op. cit.

far more intensely introverted, and divorced from ordinary everyday human existence.

He agrees that the stage of beginners contains material accessible to a psychologist, but when the mystic enters the first dark night[4] 'he has passed beyond the stage of what occurs in a normal case of even deep analysis.' In consequence, he points out, the psychologist is '. . . not very likely to meet with the mystical cases met by St. John in his own person and those of the religious for whom he wrote' (pp. 29–30). Thus Father Sumner can make a clear distinction between psychology and mysticism on theoretical and technical grounds: mystical theology is solely the province of the priest.

Now Jung, as is well known, has frequently made psychological studies of mysticism, thus taking a more extended view of the psychologist's province. He says of the relation between psychologist and priest:[5]

I must acknowledge with gratitude that the co-operation I had so long wished and hoped for has now become a reality. The present book bears witness to this, for it meets the preoccupation of medical psychology half-way, not only with intellectual understanding, but also with good will. Only an uncritical optimism could expect such an encounter to be love at first sight. The *points de départ* are too far apart for this and the road to the meeting-place too long as well as too hard to hope for agreement as a matter of course. If I am not mistaken, however, one of the main difficulties lies in the fact that both appear to speak the same language, but that this language calls up in their minds two totally different fields of associations. Both can apparently use the same concept and are then bound to acknowledge, to their amazement, that they are speaking of two different things.

This statement leads to some conclusions: we should beware of transposing psychological concepts to the theological sphere and vice versa, but this does not put any part of one discipline outside the comprehension of the other; it is only necessary to distinguish 'two fields of association'. Further, since the differences between the two disciplines may be valuable, they should not be blunted, with the idea of uniting the religious and psychological points of view by undue emphasis on the common ground.

[4] Ibid., p. 17.
[5] Foreword to Victor White, *God and the Unconscious*. London, 1952, pp. xvi–xvii.

To return to Father Sumner's formulations: in setting out his ideas he has made for clarity, but there are points which need critical comment. Consider the phrase 'grace waits, as a rule, for nature to be put in order'. Psychologists are now studying nature (i.e. human nature) and are beginning to know something about it, just as they are beginning to know something about individuation. Both these are fields of study and not matters which can be 'put in order', since it is the order in nature which is under consideration. At once we hit on that difference of association to which Jung refers.

It is not at all certain that St. John is aiming at a form of wholeness. As we have seen,[6] his is certainly a higher goal, but it differs from individuation, the form of wholeness closest to mysticism. It may be tempting at this point to agree to Father Sumner's distinction, but the evidence makes that distinction improbable; it does not appear very likely that the two can really complement each other and fit together so neatly as Father Sumner thinks.

In my earlier paper I pointed out that St. John handled material produced by a nun in a manner calculated to reinforce the repressive trends in the nun and that, in doing so, he acted in direct opposition to the manner in which an analyst would behave under comparable circumstances.

The passage to which he refers is that about the 'Judgement given by the Blessed Father upon the Spirituality and Method of Procedure in Prayer of a Nun of our Order.'[7] St. John had been asked how to handle some questionable spiritual experiences of the nun, and he takes a very negative view of them. He lists the following defects in them:

She has great desire for possession; (2) She has overmuch confidence and too few misgivings lest she stray interiorly; (3) She seems anxious to persuade others to believe that her experiences are good and abundant; (4) There seems to be no signs of humility . . .; (5) The style and language which she here uses do not seem in agreement with the spirituality to which she here lays claim.

In conclusion he says: 'All this that she says about what she said to God, and what God said to her, seems to be nonsense.' His prescription is as follows:

[6] Cf. 'The Dark Night of the Soul', see above, pp. 130 ff.
[7] *The Complete Works of Saint John of the Cross*, trans. E. Allison Peers, Vol. III. London, 1953, p. 279.

She should be neither ordered nor permitted to write anything about such things as these, nor should her confessor give any appearance of wishing to hear about them, save in order to deprecate them. Let her be tested in the practice of the virtues alone, and especially in self-contempt, humility and obedience. Such acid tests will result in the purification of her soul, which has received so many favours. But the tests must be severe, for there is no evil spirit that will not undergo some degree of suffering to his own honour.

On this Father Sumner comments on pp. 27–8 of his pamphlet:

The situation is, that St. John is showing why he considers the experiences of a certain nun, who claimed to hold long conversations with God, not to be mystical phenomena, i.e. the results of the working of the 'divine ray' on her soul. What is St. John trying to discover? It is precisely the presence of the ray of darkness. So he immediately applies the method of repression. He knows very well that, if one is forced to repress, then the material repressed into the unconscious will presently start to stink, and the smell will be noticed by all about us. If, on the other hand, the soul is being led by God, then no attempt at repression will do her any harm. So he advises that this test should be applied to the nun. If, after a good period of trials of humility and obedience, great gentleness of soul comes forth, then we may be quite sure that God is working there. This seems to me to be perfectly sound. The psychotherapist who is not looking for the working of divine grace, will not approach the case in the same manner. He will value the dialogues of the good nun with God and others as giving him matter for analytical procedure.

The repressive content of the mystical religious life is here cogently justified by Father Sumner, starting from the idea that the mystical and therefore religious man can and does use repression in the clear belief that its use can lead to a wholeness 'infinitely surpassing that of individuation'. From the analyst's point of view, however, his statement is inadequate, but to show why, it will be necessary to consider the subject of repression in more detail.

As a concept, repression is an abstraction which implies structures and energies within the psyche; it is part and parcel of the model used to define the psychodynamic processes. The concept has the qualities of psychological concepts in general in that they do not, as is too commonly assumed, give a true picture of what happens in the psyche. A conceptual model is built to orientate ourselves amongst observed phenomena; it helps to bring order into our observations and so is useful in communicating what has been discovered. It can also lead to our asking new questions and devising new ways of handling psychic events. These theoretical models correspond more or less closely to dogma in religion while they partake of the quality of scientific theories in that they can be modified in the face of new observations.

Repression is a theoretical concept whose essential definition has remained constant, but has been modified and developed in many respects.[8] It belongs to the sphere of ego psychology, and was originated by Freud because of the way in which disagreeable memories were kept from becoming conscious; symptoms and behaviour replaced the memory. This led to the idea that there was a structure within the psyche which aimed at keeping the disagreeable memories out of consciousness, out of relation to the ego, and to the definition which has remained stable; repression is a mechanism which aims at keeping particular psychic contents out of consciousness.

At first Freud seems to have laid most emphasis on the ideas kept out of consciousness, then he considered repression in terms of misrepresentation of feelings, and finally he took up its emotional meaning.

'We remain on the surface so long as we treat only of memories and ideas. The only valuable things in psychic life are, rather, the emotions. . . . Ideas are repressed only because they are connected with liberations of emotions.'

So repression was conceived as 'the inhibition of the capacity for emotional experience'.[9]

The case Jung cites of a neurotic student[10] who brought an elaborate analysis of his condition and then asked Jung why he was not cured, illustrates the importance of emotion. Jung found that the student had omitted from his record a fact which was

[8] In what follows I have drawn extensively on Madison, 'Freud's Repression Concept', *International Journal of Psycho-Analysis*, Vol. XXXVII, No. 1, 1956.

[9] Ibid., pp. 78–9.

[10] Cf. *The Development of Personality* (Collected Works, Vol. XVII). London and New York, 1954, pp. 98 f.

known to him, to wit, that the young man was letting a girl friend with little money pay for his holiday at great sacrifice to herself. When Jung pointed this out the man pooh-poohed the idea, reasoned his behaviour away and departed. What had been repressed here? Certainly not memories, but rather a whole set of highly charged feelings, all sense that he was doing something despicable; he has isolated the facts from his feeling, and Jung took the view that he was therefore suffering from a compulsion neurosis. It will be observed that this is what the doctrine of the *privatio boni* does.[11] It states that the facts of evil are not in question, but that they are due to an absence of good, and so diminishes their importance; this would appear to be why Jung has attacked the doctrine with so much vigour. It is interesting that a comparable theory exists in psychology: it states that the infant is good and loving and that the aggressive elements in human nature are due to frustration, i.e. an absence of love. Therefore all that needs to be done is to bring up the child lovingly and without frustration; then his original goodness will continue into adult life, an unfortunate idea which drives parents to distraction, leads teachers to renounce their adult status, and abandons children to their own anxieties which they do not know how to handle alone, causes them undesirable suffering and distorts their growth.

As the concept of repression continued to be used, it became more complex, and new sub-concepts were added. The innumerable thoughts, feelings, sensations, intuitions, emotions, and affects of which the psyche is made up make it impossible to imagine how they could exist together without some mechanism for selection at any particular moment.

[11] In discussing the *privatio boni* Father Hostie takes up the following position. Though theology and psychology have a common phenomenology, the conclusions drawn by the two disciplines have no relation to each other. Thus he can resolve the conflict between the two disciplines: the psychological conclusions are valid only for psychology, the theological ones only for theology. This position is neat, but it would appear to run the risk of making psychologists think that it will result in the ultimate dissolution of theology altogether, since the theological position is a human one and as such is a psychological fact. Though I cannot say I would agree with this psychological view, it does illustrate what I do believe: it is an illusion to believe that branches of knowledge can be thus separated out. (Cf. Hostie, *Religion and the Psychology of Jung* London and New York, 1957.)

Jung has elaborated the concept of opposites to include four complementary functions comprising two pairs of opposites. These opposites cannot function together; thus thinking and feeling cannot be in consciousness together; therefore if you want to think, feeling must be repressed,[12] and vice versa. Similarly in the case of sensation and intuition. Perhaps more striking still is Jung's assertion that it is in the nature of any statement about the psyche to imply a contradiction which itself proves the relative correctness of a particular thesis, i.e. it is relatively valid if it can be contradicted. Therefore if any definite view is put forward and defended against opposition, repression is necessarily taking place. These considerations show that a variety of different mechanisms must be deployed at different times and so the theory grew to fit the accumulation of observations. As the concept developed it became allied to those of ego defence and ego protection, which were soon used alongside the idea of repression, and the techniques employed by the ego were enumerated by psycho-analysts: isolation, undoing, reaction formation (or compensation), projection, substitution, reversal, conversion, etc.

From the foregoing it will be evident that repression was soon conceived as a general, even universal, mechanism. It is not in itself necessarily desirable or undesirable, though Baynes[13] says that 'repression is a fundamental necessity of biological economy', and continues: 'this is proved by the existence of the rigid sex taboo in primitive peoples.'[14] And again, 'Repression, in fact, is an innate tendency . . .' These quotations indicate clearly the view that repression is inevitable in any society, and the enormous influence of the incest taboo in the development of religious forms has been laid bare by Jung in his *Symbols of Transformation* and in many other publications as well.

Jung, furthermore, clearly infers that it must come into the individuation process when he conceives it as the consequence of conflict between the ego and the archetypes. In this conflict the ego must inevitably defend and protect itself, for otherwise it

[12] A distinction has been made between suppression, which is a deliberate conscious act, and repression, which is due to unconscious processes. I have not accepted this distinction because it does not hold water when tested against experience except in a limited number of cases.

[13] 'Freud versus Jung', *Analytical Psychology and the English Mind*. London, 1950, p. 102.

[14] i.e., the incest taboo.

would be overwhelmed and then individuation would not come about.

We may perhaps interpolate here that there is nothing necessarily bad about repression, but it has got a bad name. This is not so much because of the success of repression as because of its failure:[15] when it fails a manifest disturbance in the psyche results[16] which may take the form of one of the classes of mental disorder with which psychiatrists are familiar, and then the repressed contents demand to be investigated so that a more satisfactory arrangement of them can be brought about. Although as a concept repression is not bad, the dynamic element related to it is the feeling of an evil; it indicates the affects conceived to be dangerous by the ego, which accordingly defends and protects itself against them.

It follows that repression is not essentially pathological, indeed it extends right into the whole structure of society and into Christianity itself. That is why psychology can only say of Father Sumner's statement, that the repressive prescription was 'completely in order', that it is incomplete. But if St. John had known about our psychological model and wanted to use it as Father Sumner does, he would have need to give more consideration to what had happened in terms of the model. A doubt would have arisen in his mind, and if he wanted to collaborate with psychologists he would have found it necessary to give more detailed information when, for instance, he says that there 'will come forth that gentleness of soul in which graces so great have been wrought'. Psychologists will want to know more. The gentleness which he hoped to elicit would need to be estimated by him in terms of the concept of reaction formation. Since, however, he did not know of this concept but based his estimate on his own frame of reference he assumed that the gentleness is *essentially* good because, if I understand correctly, it conforms to the Christian virtues. Now, if we follow Jung's psychological argument in 'Answer to Job',[17] reaction formation, sometimes called over-compensation, is found to be an essential content of Chris-

---

[15] St. John's manœuvre, if it turned out as he expected, must clearly be classed as a success.

[16] Father Sumner's idea of a 'stink' would refer to this.

[17] *Psychology and Religion*: *West and East* (Collected Works, Vol. XI). London and New York, 1958.

tianity. This he brings out particularly clearly when he throws into relief the elaborate precautions against the wiles of satan which preceded the birth of Jesus. The immaculate conception and the virgin birth are manifestations of the reaction in god[18] to the realization that Job's consciousness has put man in a morally superior position to god. In his aim to become man, god is only partially successful and over-compensates, the result being a completely good image of god. This necessarily involves the erection of defences against satan, making him far more evil than before. This splitting Jung traces into the psychology of St. John, the author of the Epistles, who as a completely good bishop exemplifies the consequences of the reaction formation of which the Book of Revelation is the inevitable consequence.

Though Jung has put forward his essay as his own personal reaction, this strikes me as less unscientific and subjective than he asserts. He does not apply the concepts of repression and ego defence, which can, however, very well be used to illuminate the structure and functioning of our society and Christian religious beliefs.

We have got far enough to see how the test which Father Sumner suggests that St. John used, can be understood in the light of present psychological theory. St. John supported the repressive forces in the nun on the grounds of his wide experience, and if Father Sumner says that it is because he is looking for the 'Divine ray', the statement falls within his theological web of association. To us it would seem that St. John, by reinforcing the ego defences of the nun against the supposed works of the devil, initiated a positive reaction formation.

Let us now turn to the behaviour of analysts which I contrasted with that of St. John. To do this it is necessary to look at the basic assumptions upon which analysis rests. Analysis began from a view of science which may be stated as follows: there are scientific laws in nature which can be discovered and tested against objective observation and experiment. The laws of nature can be expressed by theoretical models which are true within their frame of reference and can be made to conform more and more closely to the natural law, assumed to exist in

---

[18] The small 'g' is used when the term 'god' is used in its psychological frame of reference. The same applies to the personal pronoun 'his'.

nature, by the interaction of new observations with the theo-retical model. This scientific attitude was combined with a therapeutic one which deliberately left the patients free to experiment with their own natures.

Psycho-analysis began by observing the free flow of speech under simple but definite conditions; the patient was asked to lie on a couch and say whatever came into his mind. The material revealed and the manner of expressing it were observed, and theories were developed which could be checked against the observations. In this way, it was found that free associations were not arbitrary, but were controlled by unconscious processes, many, though not all, of which were kept unconscious by repres-sive influences. By continuing free association and by com-municating the theories (interpretations) to the patient, these unconscious contents could be brought into consciousness and so the theories could be tested, confirmed, or disproved.

The same scientific assumptions lay behind Jung's early psychiatric studies, his association experiments, his disagree-ments with Freud, and his employment of such techniques as active imagination.[19] The early researches assumed the objec-tivity of the analyst as an axiom, but as the relation between analyst and patient gradually became the subject of more and more careful investigation, it was found that the analyst could not always be considered as objective, and the idea of counter-transference came to be formulated; it implied the idea of non-interference and non-direction of the patient's life.

Elsewhere I have discussed the nature of counter-transfer-ence[20] and have attempted to open the way to its further under-standing by defining two kinds of unconscious reaction by the analyst, the analyst's illusions about the patient and the syntonic reactions to him: the latter being reactions within the analyst which, being based on archetypal responses having objective validity, are syntonic with those of the patient.

Where these considerations lead may be illustrated by analys-ing one part of Father Sumner's account of the conditions under which the mystical process develops.

Some of his statements would inevitably be questioned in the

<hr/>

[19] Cf. above, pp. 67 ff.
[20] 'Notes on the Transference', *New Developments in Analytical Psychology*. London, 1957.

light of modern developments in knowledge, for instance, it is improbable that anybody can 'put aside solicitude about money, fortune and ambition'[21] with quite the certainty that Father Sumner seems to assume.[22] But this type of problem is a side issue; the essential point of difference is brought to the fore by the statement that the mystic puts himself 'under a Master of some kind, so that he now follows the guidance and directions of another, instead of having to try all sorts of experiments for himself.'

An analytical patient certainly puts himself under an analyst, who corresponds to the Master; the directives of the priest correspond to the right and wrong ways of conducting analyses, and in each case there are aims which differ not so much in their nature, though even here the differences are considerable, but in the method employed to achieve them. St. John without doubt conducted an experiment, whose outcome he dares to predict. In doing so, however, he overrules the possibility of the nun herself making experiments with her own life and finding out for herself whether the experiences are valid or not. This would be the method of the analyst, and it would be in the front of his mind when he stopped short at interpreting the material with the aim of mobilizing the ego or sorting out the relation of the ego to the unconscious. All this is done within the transference, and it is here that the first experiments are made by the patient before applying those that have proved successful in his everyday life. It is within the transference that the role of the "master" features, and it is one of the more interesting projections to handle because it contains a basis of truth and it can therefore become part of the syntonic counter-transference.[23] A concept of how its resolution may take place can be formulated only if we base it upon the following consideration: since human beings are individual, nobody can know ultimately what is right for another person, and so each person is the master of his own life. Therefore all that an analyst can do is to put his patient in the best position to make

---

[21] Cf. Oswald Sumner, op. cit., p. 12.

[22] Cf. Fordham, 'Biological Theory and the Concept of Archetypes' in *New Directions in Analytical Psychology*. There will be found quoted an excerpt from a mystical experience of Mechthild of Magdeburg in which these motives became the source of a struggle with a Devil.

[23] Cf. 'Notes on the Transference', op. cit.

his own experiments. It is assumed that there is no general concept of development which is ultimately right or wrong; consequently the whole idea of good and evil becomes far more relative, more psychic and more individual than Father Sumner contends that St. John asserts.

To set out the difference conceptually gives, unfortunately, little idea of the affective nature of the issues involved, for such a position cannot be reached without working through in detail the numerous anxieties about what is evil; anxieties are inevitable if the values imposed by the 'Master', i.e. the parental figure, cease to be absolute and become relative. A radical working through in the transference and counter-transference is involved: just as the patient goes through the process, so does the analyst who is only in a better position to handle the experiences as they arise because he has already experienced his own version of them.

If analysts have found a good way of dealing with many evils, they do not dispose of them. They have only developed new techniques which have proved effective on numerous occasions.

I have chosen the topic of repression because so many of the difficulties encountered in the analysis of patients can be explained by using this concept. If it were not for these difficulties, all the laborious detailed work, the necessity for long analyses, the frequent meetings of analysts and patients, the tortuous paths of transference analysis would be virtually unnecessary. The problem of repression is not often discussed by analytical psychologists because it is so much connected with ego psychology, and this has only recently begun to receive the attention it deserves. But it has always been in the forefront of analytical practice, and it is usually only through investigating it that we arrive at the archetypal forms which, under the leadership of the ego, set the stage for individuation.

There is a characteristic preliminary statement in the papers on religion written by analytical psychologists: it says that the analyst speaks as one outside the Church. Mrs. Allenby, for instance, in 'Jung's Contribution to the Religious Problem of our Time', says that her theme 'concerns those people who are no longer safely contained in the traditional framework of religious belief and doctrine.'[24] This raises the question of what has happened. Has the analyst ever been inside a church, and if so why

[24] Guild of Pastoral Psychology Pamphlet, No. 91, p. 5.

did he retire from it? The view that the traditional beliefs make people feel safe suggests a longing to be back again in an imaginary safe container, but I doubt whether those inside the churches really feel any safer than those outside them; indeed in listening to the public and private statements of members of the churches I sometimes think the reverse. In any case there is no firm evidence one way or the other.

Mrs. Allenby's assumption would seem to be that the aim of organized religion is to keep its members under the sway of parental figures. This is not specific for religion: when analysts organize themselves into societies, these inevitably structure themselves according to the family pattern. The tendency is a property of organizations as a whole, which, at some stages anyway, stand in the way of individual development. The aim of analytical psychologists is, however, to increase the capacity for moral autonomy and so reduce the need for parental authority and care; I cannot say that the result has been what might have been hoped for in so far as group adaptation has been tried, indeed the result is a tendency to deny infantile behaviour which is not able to reach consciousness because analysts are supposed to be mature. I hardly think analytical psychologists are in a position to be superior about the older organizations!

Jung asserts that he has successfully shepherded several individuals back into various religious denominations. There is, as far as I am aware, no account of the reverse process, which can come about as the result of loosening repressive ties. I would therefore like to conclude this paper by giving an account of such a development. I am glad to say something about this reverse process because it is feared in some quarters that analysts are rootedly opposed to religious organizations. This should not be the case, though there are some grounds for thinking that it is; if so, those who read what follows will be able to know how the worst happens.

It may perhaps be worth interpolating here that the complexity of the relation which any particular individual has with a group is such that it would be out of place to generalize. The idea that the Church can contain all the archetypal forms, and so keep people normal, seems to me thoroughly dubious,[25] as also does the

---

[25] Cf. Coulton, *Five Centuries of Religion*, Vol. I, in which many examples of neurotic priests are described. The disorders are attributed to Devils.

corollary that there is more mental disorder today because of the failure of the Church to perform its mediaeval function. These statements are far too condensed, and need critical examination by historians.

The patient was a young woman in the early thirties who was manifestly religious inasmuch as she practised her religious observances with zeal. But some of her behaviour did not accord with what would seem to be required of her by her religion. As she became aware of what her behaviour meant she started to rationalize it, but gradually it changed and she attempted to renounce it, succeeding over prolonged periods by substituting less obviously sinful activities. During this period she added to her prayers what she believed to be active imagination, producing many interesting and lively paintings and fantasies.

She made determined attempts to find out my own religious position. It was interesting to watch the ingenious way in which she tried to manœuvre me into the position of being hostile to her religion by embroiling me in discussions on metaphysics, where she was better informed, or by setting up Jungian psychology as a new kind of religion and speaking with warmth and enthusiasm of the exciting and terrible heresies of the supposed Jungian cult. This gave strong support to the idea, of which there were other indications, that her religious beliefs and practices were not secure and that their compensatory nature was not to be relied on. The 'heresies of the Jungian cult' were indications of the fantasies to which I have referred above, and to which a further interesting and relevant content may now be added: the intrusion of sexual, erotic feelings and fantasies into her religious practices in a way that reminded me of St. John's statement that 'impure acts and motions' happen 'even when the spirit is deep in prayer, to taking part in the Sacrament of Penance or in the Eucharist'.[26] These, however, were far more guilt-ridden than in the case of St. John, who regards them as often caused by the 'pleasure which human nature takes in spiritual things'.[27] He gives two other causes, Satan and fear; these latter are the analogies of those which dominated the patient, she feared them, and concealed them because she felt the evil in them.

It was these that led her to a thorough distrust of anything

[26] *The Complete Works of Saint John of the Cross*, trans. by E. Allison Peers. London, 1953, Vol. I, p. 338.   [27] Ibid., pp. 338–9.

with 'uplift' in it, and this extended not only to religion but to 'Jungian psychology' as a whole. The analysis became more and more an analysis of her instinctual life and the family patterns which lay at the roots of her becoming a member of the church, which appeared to have the characteristics mentioned by Father Sumner (p. 2): Mother Church had in a very special sense taken the part of the natural mother. This special sense could be defined as the idealized split off parts of the mother imago which were easily carried over into the religious pattern because her mother was a member of the Church.[28]

Under these circumstances it is tempting to say that her religion was false, a pathological product. This solution, however, is inadequate, since it contained much that was felt to be good, and her religious practices helped to preserve these parts of herself from the ravages of imagined evil. The patient's problem here centred on the amount of idealization to be found in the Church which fitted her psychic needs beautifully at one period in her life. It then provided what she needed, but an ideal set of virtues and an ideally good God became a great disadvantage when she began to notice that those who believe in Him behave no better than those who do not.

As the numerous repressive devices broke down, she became conscious of the motives for her beliefs, and there followed a period of progressive disillusionment so that she could not continue as before. She prayed less and less and went to fewer and fewer services. Gradually the underlying projections into her body came into view, but they could do so only by recognizing the false element in her religious activities which gradually ceased. In using the term false, I wish to underline that it was her particular psychic organization which made them so. The idealized religious forms were realized as defensive and rigid, a means of imagining she was good without really feeling that she had any good in her, i.e. her own genuinely good 'self' had become dissociated from her ego ideal.

But what had happened to her religious feeling? At one time she stated that she did not lose her sense of the presence of God but rather that He became more immanent, being within her and within others, but this gradually became less as she dared to do what Jung terms experimenting.

[28] The Church of England.

At one time the patient felt she was being handed over to the Devil, but this feeling lost ground because she realized her increasing capacity for love, greater charity and real humility, and further her capacity for enjoying life, which became more and not less meaningful, increased. All this resulted from the dissolution of projections.

In his lecture Father Sumner says (p. 27): '. . . the withdrawal of projections will occur as a result of the daily disciplined recital of the psalmody in which we meet all of the archetypal images . . .'. I think there may well be a confusion here, for recital of the psalmody does not necessarily mean that these forms contain archetypal energy. 'This people honoureth me with their lips, but their heart is far from me' may refer to the disparity between the forms and their content. Their very perfection leads to identification with them, and so keeps all sorts of sins unconscious; religious people can, and often do, deceive not only others but themselves as well, by clinging to the forms. This means that the ritual can be used for the purpose of repression and not only the kind of withdrawal of archetypal projections which leads to an increase in consciousness, for it is this to which Father Sumner seems to refer.

We here arrive at a problem of considerable complexity: the interrelation between projections consequent on the activity of ego defences, and those which are the result of the spontaneous activity of archetypes in the unconscious. Each needs very different treatment; those resulting from repression cannot be withdrawn by ritual practices; they can only be handled by going to their concealed roots. Those which are emergent preconscious images can be brought into closer relation to the ego by various means, for instance active imagination; whether the projections can be withdrawn 'as a result of the daily disciplined recital of the psalmody' is beyond my sphere of experience, and it is here that we might hope that Father Sumner may one day give us the evidence for which, as analysts, we look. I may remark, however, that if Father Sumner would modify his statement from 'will occur' to 'may occur', he would leave room for the known complexity of the problems subsumed under the heading of 'the withdrawal of projections', and would give more recognition to the psychological issues at stake.

I am far from thinking that the motives which led my patient to loosen her ties with the Church could not equally well apply to analytical psychology as a body of knowledge with technical methods and standards of its own. In fact all the projections she made into the Church could be made into analytical psychology —indeed they happened within the transference, but did not become fixed. It is not difficult to idealize the archetypal forms and analytical techniques; it can be done with active imagination in which some special virtue is supposed to reside; previously dream analysis had this status. When faced with the problem of evil, difficulties will arise: then individuation can be evoked in the belief that everything will somehow come all right; accordingly everybody wants to individuate because it is a good thing, therefore all imagination gets called active imagination, including the play of children. Next everybody who can imagine the right symbols is supposed to be individuating, and those who have little imagination get quite a false sense of inferiority. All the tricks in the world can be played if the analyst forgets that his primary aim is the analysis of a person, and that all the dreams and imaginings can be just as much misused as well used by him.

Jung recently published a commentary on the Trickster figure.[29] It bears closely on the content of repression, and points to the importance of humour and even ridicule in the history of the Church as exemplified in the various feasts against which the Church has been compelled to defend herself through conciliar decrees. Jung here defines the trickster figure as the shadow, but he also relates it to Mercurius who combines the opposites in himself and is closely related to the self.[30]

This most suggestive analysis gives repression a purposive meaning, which could be translated into the now accepted view that its investigation leads to greater wholeness. But it indicates more than a technical discovery in pointing to an inner unconscious process which, if raised to a more conscious level and there wrestled with, will take on a purposive character and initiate individuation.

This purposive element may be compared to Father Sumner's idea that St. John used repression as a test to detect the divine

[29] Cf. Paul Radin, *The Trickster*. London, 1956.
[30] Ibid., and also J. Layard, *Journal of Analytical Psychology*, Vol. II, No. 1, pp. 106 f.

ray, but the great difference still remains between St. John's making the experiment on the nun and my patient's doing it herself without authoritative guidance but only with interpretative assistance. The comparison necessarily blurs the theologian's sharp line of division between mysticism and psychology.

We have so far considered how my patient's sense of the immanence of God was increased at the same time as she left the Church. It would not surprise me, however, if her sense of God's immanence were to diminish or even disappear should she continue her development along the lines I have described. Then it might be said that she had lost her religion, but it might also be the confirmation of a hypothesis comparable to that of St. John: all that she said and felt about God proved to be erroneous. This would be what a theologian might legitimately say; as a psychologist I would put it differently by stating that as her projections originating in infancy became withdrawn she increased her capacity to take responsibility for her life, becoming increasingly mature and morally autonomous. How these two statements interdigitate is important. If both were correct there would be little problem; but are they?

In its early stages analytical psychology was a technique of psychotherapy, but it has now gone far towards giving up the limited aim from which it started. While it should adhere to scientific criteria, it has, without doubt, much to learn from theology. It would appear that, as therapeutic aims are superseded, analyses tend to become longer and longer, whilst their aim becomes less and less therapeutic and more and more like that of pure research.

As the older psychotherapeutic system the Church would seem to possess understanding in this realm. She contends that religious observances should continue for the whole of life. She also maintains a humility and tolerance of her many failures, a virtue analysts might cultivate. I feel sure that these manifestations rest on knowledge which analysts need.

To conclude, I wish to emphasize that my aim has been to keep open the doors between analytical psychology and religion. I realize that the relation between the two disciplines is only at its beginning, and if I have been critical I hope this will be taken in the constructive spirit in which it is meant.

If some religious people find, in my examples, confirmation of their worst fears, it will yet show them what may happen and on what grounds one analyst at least feels that it was all in the patient's best interest. If that be so he cannot imagine that God would be displeased at it.

XI

ANALYTICAL PSYCHOLGY AND PSYCHOTHERAPY[1]

INTRODUCTION

PSYCHOTHERAPY can be defined as any technique which aims at removing undesirable or pathological symptoms originating in the psyche, and it is sometimes held that any technique, whether it be physical, psychic, or spiritual, can be applied for this purpose. Symptom removal is, however, increasingly recognized as a poor criterion of cure, and interest has tended to shift from it to the more radical question of how therapeutic changes are brought about at all. The science of analytical psychology can hope to contribute towards this problem. Its aim of investigating dynamic phenomena may expect to result in contributions to the formation of a general theory of therapy as well as to evolving and evaluating techniques of investigation.

At the present time it is difficult to define criteria of cure, let alone to assess the value of any treatment with precision; it is indeed easier to state what is not good therapy rather than what is. Thus it can often be said that, even though a result may appear gratifying on the surface, it is likely to be unstable. Such knowledge is mainly derived from the fact that, when the personality is studied as a whole, the patient can pass through stages which are manifestly neurotic or even psychotic before stability is reached. These conditions may well became apparently cured in the course of analysis without either the analyst or the patient considering the result final.

[1] This paper was originally published as part of a symposium on Mental Health in the *British Medical Bulletin*, Vol. VI, Parts 1–2, 1949. It has been considerably revised but its essential nature has not been altered. I have attempted to state what is agreed amongst analytical psychologists, and have to a considerable extent repressed my own individual views.

168

In stating that analytical psychology can contribute to the theory of psychotherapy it is necessary to point out that analytic concepts can be applied whether the procedure under consideration be long or short. Therapy is basically a question not of time, but of how the needs of a patient can best be met. The demand for short therapies, which used to be heard more often than it is today, is peculiar to psychotherapy. In other types of medical treatment, in which the disparity between the number of doctors and the number of patients requiring treatment has not been so marked, time is scarcely mentioned. It is the recognition of the wide extent of mental disorder that has led to a demand that something be done. If less time is spent on each patient more patients can be assisted; this is the main argument behind the cry for short treatments. It may be expected to sink into the background as facilities for treatment increase.

Whether the treatment be long or short, there is one great advantage in the therapist's having undertaken long analyses: in this way alone can he appreciate what can and what cannot be done. A long analysis puts therapeutic possibilities in perspective and reveals more convincingly than anything else what psychotherapy cannot do. It reveals the fact that there is often just as much to be said for not treating a patient as there is for starting a therapy under conditions which are not sufficiently favourable.

But time, which can often be found, is not so difficult a problem as that of money, of which some patients, who could otherwise be treated, have not enough to make it possible for analysts to accept them for analysis. If analysts took on all the potential patients who could not pay reasonable fees they would soon be poverty-stricken.

Undoubtedly one factor in the length of treatment is the high value placed on the individual by analysts. There are cases in which the individuality is so important that not only is a long time necessary, but methods, as commonly conceived, have to be, if not eliminated, at least reduced to a minimum.[2] But it is not only these rather special cases which need such individual consideration, it applies to all of them, and Jung's conclusion that amongst primitive people '. . . a single human being is never considered unique, but is always interchangeable with any other and

[2] Cf. Jung, 'Principles of Practical Psychotherapy', *The Practice of Psychotherapy* (Collected Works, Vol. XVI). London and New York, 1954.

is easily dispensible'[3] is worth reflecting upon. Methods of treatment claiming general validity lead to a corresponding devaluation of the individual, especially when they are intended to apply to anyone suffering from any class of mental disorder. The days of a general panacea are, however, over; yet a modified version of them can often be discerned in the application of the medical idea of a therapy which can be applied to a disease entity. If diseases are treated as entities, then the individual as a unique person cannot be considered.

In what follows I intend to give some account of the analytical procedures and of the knowledge which has been accumulated from the practice of them, which are likely to have significance for those whose immediate interest is the less radical healing of psychogenic disorders. Amongst these we may mention firstly psychiatrists, particularly those working in out-patient clinics, who undoubtedly have the most difficult job because of the pressure of patients, lack of time, and the need to bring treatments to a conclusion; secondly, general practitioners, who have the advantage of having the patients under their constant care, knowing their environment, and being able to watch their development; thirdly, the clergy, who have behind them an organized ritual and ethical pattern to which the moral problems of the members of their congregations can be referred. It would, I think, be quite wrong if the members of these social groups tried to apply the principles of analytical practice to anything but a minute sample of the individuals under their care. Analytic knowledge, however, can give them means of access to human nature which they can adapt to their conditions of work.

THE ANALYST'S PERSONALITY

To use suggestion in the form of interpretation based on theoretical presuppositions[4] is likely to be effective when social maladaptation is important or when the patient is too remote from the instinctual basis of his life and needs to be related to it. The method should, however, be regarded as a tool in the hands of a physician. Method is subsidiary to the way he, as a human

---

[3] 'Archaic Man', *Modern Man in Search of a Soul*. London, 1933, p. 171.

[4] Cf. Jung, 'Principles of Practical Psychotherapy', op. cit.

being, uses it; his personality is conceived in analytical psychology as the main therapeutic factor.[5] In minor psychotherapy it may well be overlooked; it cannot be avoided in a thorough analysis, for sooner or later, it will be clear that the important therapeutic factor is to be found not only in the patient's personality but also in that of the physician. These interact in any case, but in a long analysis any method based on theoretical presuppositions becomes subsidiary to the personality of the analyst, which then interacts openly with that of the patient in what is termed the dialectical relationship.

Analytical psychology has always placed a personal analysis in the centre of its requirements for the training of analysts. This aims at raising consciousness to the level which can reasonably be expected of the candidate, for free interaction with a patient is dangerous without a high degree of capacity to regulate what happens. To interact openly requires very considerable maturity, otherwise it will lead to unfortunate, even disastrous results.[6]

Once the analysis is completed it cannot, however, be assumed that the analyst is without blemish. This is one reason why he sits facing, or beside, his patient; the couch is seldom used, though some consider it valuable. Sitting in view of the patient ensures that he can make observations by using his eyes as well as his ears. The sitting position in full view of the subject also expresses the analyst's willingness to treat him as an equal, even though, because of the transference, the patient may not believe this to be the case. Lastly, this position indicates the analyst's willingness to react to the patient's material and reveal himself. It is these last requirements above all which make it essential for the analyst to be aware of himself, and sufficiently integrated to be capable of knowing and tolerating his own unintegrated states. On the face of it, unintegrated responses look undesirable, but so long as they are recognized as such they can be therapeutic. Concealed inferiorities can fascinate and hinder the analytical development because they cannot be seen but only vaguely felt as unexplained consequences of the hidden complex within the analyst.

[5] Cf. Jung, 'The Therapeutic Value of Abreaction', *The Practice of Psychotherapy*.

[6] Cf. Kraemer, 'The Dangers of Unrecognized Counter-Transference', *Journal of Analytical Psychology*, Vol. III, No. 1, 1958.

The view that the analyst's personality is the vital factor in analytical practice extends to everything he says or does, since these activities reveal his personality and its degree of development. Interpretations show his insight and understanding, and are not just technical manœuvres which can be learnt; rather they are in the first place expressions of his own experience which has been worked through and integrated in his own life. But each time, even if they be typical interpretations of situations which have often arisen before, they cannot avoid being expressions of his relation to a particular patient. They remain individual on each occasion, and would be individual even if the only unique feature were the timing of the statement.

THE TRANSFERENCE

It will now be clear that understanding of the transference cannot be based upon the concept that the analyst is a mere screen upon which the patient projects unconscious contents, though this he will often do, behaving as if the analyst were a screen. Taken as a whole, however, he is a reacting person, but he may be expected to be more experienced, more integrated, and more capable of tolerating and understanding unintegrated states of his psyche than is the patient. Therefore the transference must be conceived as an interaction between two personalities. This concept is based *au fond* upon that of the archetypes, whose transpersonal nature ensures that the analyst is himself affected when these become active. Once again the importance of the analysis of the analyst is illustrated, for without this essential initiation he will not know how to handle these problems and may indeed get into the position of not even realizing the effect an archetype is having upon him. In the face of them he is only too liable to pile up defensive explanations of the patient's behaviour, which are unconsciously designed to cover a counter-transference illusion.

The interaction between analyst and patient has been, and is continuing to be, subjected to investigation from the viewpoint of analytical psychology. Jung's essay on the transference[7] has

[7] 'Psychology of the Transference', *The Practice of Psychotherapy*, pp. 161 ff. Cf. also Fordham, 'Notes on the Transference', *New Developments in Analytical Psychology*. London, 1957.

greatly stimulated this research. In the essay cited Jung shows how the conscious mind and the unconscious of the two parties interact. He goes into the contrasexual relation which develops in the unconscious if the pair be of opposite sexes. In the conscious the man relates to a woman as a man to a woman, but in the unconscious a reversal takes place: the man's anima comes into relation with the animus of the woman. It is through this unconscious conjunction that the self emerges into consciousness.[8]

The essence of the whole analytic procedure, its success or failure, clearly depends upon the analyst's capacity to meet the patient. He may do this with understanding at one time, with affect at another. Some of the differences between analyst and patient have already been enumerated; to these may be added the analyst's greater plasticity, which makes it possible to unravel resistances and meet his own affective archetypal experiences as evoked by the patient's unconscious. Thus in any thoroughgoing analysis the transference is the core of the whole proceeding. Within it the patient is able to re-experience past events which have resulted in fixations and also new, never before experienced, archetypal events. The processes of self-realization come from these two classes of experience.

It follows that the analyst's unconscious is a highly significant factor in all analyses, and analysts need to keep it in mind that at some time or other the patient will be able to reveal aspects of the analyst's nature of which he himself has no knowledge. Consequently to deny an observation by a patient, even though it appears to be a projection, is a hazardous proceeding. Fortunately this denial can usually be avoided till it is relatively meaningless.

A further consequence is that no good analyst will come out of an analysis unchanged. This must be so because of the intensity of the experience and of the fact that the patient will reveal some aspect or other of the analyst of which the latter was unconscious.

It is often held that the success of a therapy depends upon the psychotherapist's belief in his method; analytical psychology can contribute to the theory of this view. If it be understood that the

[8] Clearly many other forms of transference can be described and enumerated. The reader is referred to the volume cited and the literature as a whole to which reference is made in my own paper, ibid.

belief is founded upon one archetype, then it will at once be clear that it simply links his technique with the affective part of his personality, and so he affects his patient unconsciously as well as with his conscious intention.

THE PATTERN OF ANALYSIS

In the light of analytical theory the pattern of an ideal analysis is made up of three stages. The first is confession of material already conscious, proceeding to clarification of subliminal material, day dreams, etc.

When this material has been ventilated and interpreted, there begins the second stage: the analysis of the repressed unconscious. This consists in unearthing memories and past experiences which have not yet been resolved, and in the clarification of personal feelings which, through the action of repression, have not been allowed to come into consciousness. This inevitably leads to the instinctual basis of the psychic organism.

As this process goes on, we begin to see the archetypes of the collective unconscious emerging, at first hidden behind the personal experience and then coming more and more into the open; this indicates the onset of the third stage. The classical analysis now develops as a dialectic in which the process of transformation begins; it releases the patient more and more from the analyst owing to the operation of the individuation process.

We can view this typical or ideal analytical process as part of the whole development of an individual life, which gradually unfolds itself as the years go on, for the age of the patient is of essential significance as a guide to the conduct of psychotherapy. Jung has described the individuation process as a phenomenon of the second half of life, i.e. one that starts between thirty-five and forty years of age. At this stage the ego is conceived as firmly established, and so the individual is able to give libido to the problems of the living process of which he is in a sense the representative; the process becomes transpersonal. During the first half of life, on the contrary, the problem centres first of all round the development of the ego in connexion with personal relationships, as a preparation for more independent living. For this purpose the parents are necessary containers of the child's existence. When the child becomes a man or woman, the problem changes, and becomes how to achieve sufficient independence of the parents, to work, earn a living, marry, and found a family—in a word, social adaptation. When this is done, what next? A peak has been reached, after which begins a gradual descent to old age and death; it is a period of increasing introversion. At this peak, a change occurs which heralds the increasing need for revision and reflection upon the problems of life as a whole as experienced by the individual; in other words, the problem of individuation comes to the fore. It is to this period that analytical psychology has made its special contribution.

If we consider the therapeutic problems in the light of these observations, we arrive at the conclusion that different periods of life demand different kinds of attitude. In the first half the problems are predominantly personal, and in consequence the therapeutic process will centre round the repressed unconscious; in the second half, the collective unconscious will contain the essential problem of individuation. Our scheme will therefore serve as a guide to be taken in conjunction with the stage of life through which the individual is passing.

But in all these stages any therapeutic manœuvre needs to be conducted so as not to interfere with the next—for each is part of the process which may be termed self-realization, and in it all the self will be operative. Thanks to Jung, this can be perceived through symbolic forms and found in dreams and imagination, a knowledge of which is therefore necessary in order to recognize its activity when its symbolism appears.

These considerations give longitudinal *indicia* for the analyst in terms of age. But clearly there are different kinds of people who will approach these problems differently, and the form in which the problem presents itself can vary greatly. This fact has been met in terms of various classifications. Jung met it by formulating a theory of types attempting to embrace the normal, healthy parts of the personality as well as the pathological shadow. In so doing he aimed at the same time at defining the lines along which regressions were most likely to develop.

Jung's type theory is an elaborate structure, by no means easy to understand and apply.[9] It provides the psychotherapist with

[9] In 'The Inferior Function', *Studien zur analytischen Psychologie C. G. Jungs*, Vol. I, Zurich, 1955, pp. 134 f., J. L. Henderson says: 'When an inexperienced psychotherapist begins to apply Jung's concept of

a means of determining the attitude of the conscious mind, and is therefore a stepping-stone towards differentiation, aiming at the assessment, via the attitude of the conscious mind, of the personality as a whole.

According to the theory, there are four possible functions of consciousness: two rational, *thinking* and *feeling* (valuation), and two irrational, *sensation* and *intuition*. To this already complicated structure is added the notion that the conscious attitude may be directed outwards, *extraverted*, or inwards, *introverted*. Once the attitude and function of the conscious mind has been determined, we are in a position to infer those of the unconscious, because of its complementariness to that of the conscious mind. The unconscious attitudes and functions complement that of the conscious and contain those that are neglected, undeveloped and incompatible.

A moment's reflection will show that the number of 'types' which this system will contain is large. Partly for this reason, and partly because we know that considerable modification in type is possible, it could never be used in a rigid fashion. The eight types which Jung describes in his classical work[10] make up an axial system through which one may orientate oneself amongst the variety of human beings whom the psychotherapist is bound to meet in his practice.

FREQUENCY OF INTERVIEWS

Analysts vary in their opinions regarding the frequency of interviews; moreover, the stage reached in the analysis has to be taken into consideration. Jung[11] regards four times a week as enough. In the early stages and in other critical periods of analy-

psychological types he is rather like a child who has been given a fine watch before he can read numbers accurately and before he has any idea of the significance of time beyond that associated with his immediate personal desires or needs. He can admire the precision of its craftsmanship and the gleaming metal of its case, but its actual use is fraught with subjective hazards. . . . It is no wonder then that, in spite of its popular appeal and its many possibilities in understanding, psychotherapists not trained in analytical psychology have failed to apply the type theory correctly and have frequently tried to discredit its validity altogether.'

[10] *Psychological Types*. London and New York, 1923.

[11] 'Principles of Practical Psychotherapy', *The Practice of Psychotherapy*, p. 20.

sis frequent interviews are desirable, particularly when the contents of consciousness are being confessed and when the repressed unconscious is being analysed.[12] During this period the transference is developing and is being handled on the objective plane. By this it is meant that objective situations in the past are being revealed through the transference, which has to be analysed in relation to the past.

When, however, the analysis reaches the level of the collective unconscious a different situation can begin to arise. The contents of the analytical transference become less and less personal and, provided the ego is sufficiently established and capable of adopting a suitable attitude, the subject may be expected to take increasing responsibility for the material, arising out of the unconscious, which he sees more as an inner problem of his own. This process can be fostered by the interpretations on the subject plane which bring the patient into relation with himself. These interpretations underline the synthetic processes of the analysis which have been there all the time but from now on can often predominate.

As a consequence of these reflections, and taking them into consideration with the section on the pattern of analysis, we can see that interviews may be less frequent for subjects in the second half of life.[13]

DREAM ANALYSIS, AMPLIFICATION AND ACTIVE IMAGINATION

Analytical psychology distinguishes two ways of approaching dreams. The first consists in eliciting free associations. By this means a long string of seemingly disconnected material is produced which leads to the complexes. The other method consists in determining the dream context. This is done by amplification; according to this method we need only enough association material to show the context. Two kinds of contexts can appear— the personal and the collective.

[12] The difficulty of reducing interviews is that it changes the meaning of the analysis significantly—further, once done it is not always easy to increase them again.

[13] This assessment is not to be taken as a rule; the number of interviews depends not only on the degree of maturity but also on personality type, severity of the neurosis or psychosis, intensity of anxiety aroused by the transference, and individual and interpersonal factors which cannot be classified easily, if at all.

N   177

Amplification is an extension of a natural process which has been observed in dream series. In these series, the images develop in a particular way, and refer to a central nucleus; by means of analogy the images appear as it were to revolve round it, gradually concentrating more and more upon its essential nature. Thus the material referring to the central image amplifies the central content, or throws now one, now another of its aspects into relief until a complete picture is built up and crystallizes out.

To this natural process can be added, with due respect to their transference significance, apparently artificial additions of mythological parallels by the analyst. These additions are primarily indirect statements by the analyst of his own individual experiences. The additions therefore are not made only as the result of reference to the literature, but out of the affective experience of the analyst. The use of this procedure is justified when the patient may or does become disorientated by the strangeness of the material that comes out of the unconscious.

These methods are preliminary; they precede the interpretation, which cannot be made without collecting the necessary material. When this has been done the question arises whether it needs to be understood in relation to the external or internal objects, i.e. to actual people in the environment or to internal 'persons' or archetypal images. Which interpretation is relevant depends upon the attitude of the patient's conscious mind, whether it be extraverted or introverted.

Without going further into the complications of this problem, we shall follow up the consequences of the inner development which lead to the collective unconscious. When the archetypal images come into clear relief, the process of active imagination may begin.[14]

CONCLUSION

The scientific work undertaken has complicated the psychotherapeutic field, but this complexity was certainly there in the first place. In approaching the psyche and describing its phenomena, analytical psychology claims to have contributed towards placing the psychotherapist in a position to deal more effectively

[14] Cf. 'Problems of Active Imagination', above, pp. 67 ff.

with the obscure realms with which all those engaged in that art have to contend.

The question will necessarily be raised: In what kind of cases will Jung's concepts be most useful? From what has been said, it will be clear that his work frees us from the necessity of pursuing one method alone, but rather provides us with a number of pointers which will guide the psychotherapist in his relationship to his patient.[15] Therefore this work is applicable to a wide variety of patients, but the special contribution of Jung's work is to introverted psychology and to those in the second half of life. We may say, therefore, that the introvert will naturally be more attracted than the extravert, while those who need to evaluate their lives by making original experiments, and through this to find an individual rather than a collective solution, are likely to find in analytical psychology a means of arriving at an answer to their problems.

Finally, we should not end without referring to the special contribution which analytical psychology has made to psychiatry. It has proved especially useful in cases of schizoid personality, and thus provides a means of approach to schizophrenia itself.

[15] It will be remarked that very little has been written by analytical psychologists on psychopathology proper. They are, however, bound by Jung's writings to study other analytic schools. He himself claims that he uses the researches of Freud and Adler, and his followers are therefore bound to keep abreast of and digest as far as they are able the theories and findings of the various developing schools of psycho-analysis, et al.

XII

A SUGGESTED CENTRE FOR
ANALYTICAL PSYCHOLOGY

THIS paper was read to the Analytical Psychology Club on 21 April 1944, shortly before the Society of Analytical Psychology was founded. The appeal it makes to maintain the overall unity of the Analytical Psychology Club and its analysts failed; but the division proved successful enough for the arrangement to influence societies of analysts in other countries. I still think, however, that the ideas here set out are worth putting on record. The danger of forming exclusively professional groups is that too much stress gets laid on analytical techniques, and the wider scientific impetus which gave birth to analytical psychology becomes lost to sight.

The proposal to start a centre for analytical psychology with a house in which the members of the Analytical Psychology Club could find a regular meeting place, and where there would also be a clinic, has been under consideration for some time, and I hope it will now be possible to clarify the issues and find a way to take concrete steps in the not-too-distant future. The report of the Committee concerned with the proposal will shortly be available, and will contain, first, ascertained facts, then the outline of a possible framework for the centre, and finally the Committee's unanimous recommendations.

In this paper I shall cover some, though not all, of the ground covered by the report and shall make use of some of the material in it. This, however, is incidental; my main object is to set the report in a framework, to review the development and present situation of analytical psychology especially in its relation to medicine, and then to consider some of the reasons for us analytical psychologists to organize ourselves in a more coherent and formal way. I shall end with a brief note on the shape which our society might take.

The proposal to form a centre, if it comes into force, will mean a radical change for us. It will mean a transition from one state to another, a growth from immaturity to maturity in the collective sense. Therefore I do not doubt that there will be a resistance to the very idea of anything at all happening. We all know that decisions provoke a resistance which has to be dealt with before the development can proceed; we shall all have experienced *that* in ourselves, and we all know that the objections tend to express themselves in an oblique way according to the nature of the shadow. It would be hopelessly unreal if there were no disturbance, even if the matter were handled very neatly. In this connexion I would like to quote a passage from Professor Jung's paper on 'The Psychology of the Child Archetype', for it applies aptly to our present problem.

The symptoms of compensation are described, from the progressive point of view, in scarcely flattering terms. Since, to the superficial eye, it looks like a retarding operation, people speak of inertia, backwardness, scepticism, fault-finding, conservatism, timidity, petulance, and so on. But inasmuch as man has, in high degree, the capacity for cutting himself off from his own roots, he may also be swept uncritically to catastrophe by his dangerous one-sidedness. The retarding ideal is always more primitive, more natural (in the good sense as in the bad), and more 'moral' in that it keeps faith with law and tradition. Progress enforced by will is always *convulsive*. Backwardness may be closer to naturalness, but in its turn it is always menaced by painful awakenings. The older view of things realized that progress is only possible *Deo concedente*, thus proving itself conscious of opposites, and repeating the age-old *rites d'entrée et de sortie* on a higher plane. The more differentiated consciousness becomes, the greater the danger of severance from the root-condition. Complete severance comes when the *Deo concedente* is forgotten. Now it is an axiom of psychology that when a part of the psyche is split off from consciousness it is only *apparently* inactivated; in actual fact it brings about a possession of the personality with the result that the individual's aims are falsified in the direction of the split-off part. If, then, the childhood state of the collective psyche is repressed to the point of total exclusion, the unconscious content overwhelms the conscious intention and inhibits, falsifies, even destroys its realization. Viable progress only comes from the co-operation of both.[1]

[1] In Jung and Kerenyi, *Introduction to a Science of Mythology*. London, 1951 (American edition: *Essays on a Science of Mythology*. New York, 1949). pp. 113–14.

Let us go back to the origin of the Club. Analytical psychology may be said to have begun in 1914, when Jung finally separated from Freud; that was the explosive event which has made the Club possible. It reverberated all over the psychological world and far beyond it—it rose to mythological proportions. The differences between Freud and Jung, between psychoanalysis and analytical psychology, have not been healed, and are not likely to be healed for some time to come. Differences between the analytical schools, nay, their very existence, are apparently something repugnant to a large section of the English community, and it is somehow characteristic of our nation that the largest group of psychotherapists in this country should style themselves eclectic. I think, I suppose I may dare to say we all think, however, that the advantage of belonging to a school is that we know more definitely where we stand. It may be tragic that analysts are divided up into groups, but it can also be taken to indicate the vital interest which the unconscious, as a subject of study, arouses.

To cut a long story short, we have all decided to content ourselves with the present state of affairs and have settled down to work along our own line, finding therein a fruitful existence. I should not be an analytical psychologist if the advantages of submitting to a comprehensive idea were not vastly superior. Each group has its limitations, some of them capable of alteration, some of them firm like a rock against which it is futile to protest.

One of the limitations of our group is, I think, capable of being altered. It is this: we have developed so much interest in, so much fascination for, the concept of archetypal forms in the unconscious, that the realities of the world we live in tend to be neglected; we suffer from this because the external world makes demands on groups of people which we have never seemed disposed to fulfil.

Analytical psychologists have so far mainly studied unconscious processes and a way of living which involves becoming conscious through a relation to the unconscious, expressed in the process of individuation. The phenomena of this process of individuation have been adequately presented to the world through the usual channels, and the basic concepts of analytical psychology have been stated, but they do not yet find general acceptance by any recognized collective body, consequently there is nowhere for us to fit in. The practical consequences of this are serious: there are no hospitals and scarcely any clinics in which a doctor can practise analytical psychology without continually coming up against resistances on the part of other members of the staff. Therefore, we have, if only for this reason, to try to create our own collective milieu. I know that there is the Davidson Clinic in Edinburgh which is strongly influenced by our concepts of analytical psychology and the Guild of Pastoral Psychology also has started a Clinic.[2] There are two formal societies in which analytical psychology has considerable influence; these are the Guild of Pastoral Psychology, of which Jung is president, and the Oxford Psychology and Religion Society. In addition there are smaller informal groups in other areas, for instance, one which Mrs. Champernowne has formed in Exeter.[3]

It is conceivable that this is the way we should grow, namely by forming societies which are inspired by our concepts but do not bear our name, and have two roots, one as it were in Zurich, another in religion, or medicine, or anthropology, or so on. It would, however, be unfortunate if the psychological standpoint which Jung has formulated, and which we regard as fundamental, were not given separate expression in an effective and open way.

It is the one which the Analytical Psychology Club has for more than twenty years represented with consistency; that is one justification for its existence. It is the only body which uses the name analytical psychology and which stands by its origin. It has shown a progressive growth, and has done much pioneer work in its own field. It has held lectures at regular intervals and has welcomed in its midst many eminent lecturers, not only analysts, and so has not been excessively exclusive. It has developed Jung's methods of investigating the unconscious, has held study groups, and has built up the nucleus of a good library. It has also had its social side, in the form of periodic meetings, in which members could get to know each other.

The question of making a concerted effort to do more in an extraverted field had for some time been in the minds of members. It was certainly considered at the time that I was Chairman of the Club, and before the war a series of public lectures were given under the chairmanship of Dr. de Laszlo. They were well

[2] It was only in existence for a short time.   [3] The Withymead Centre.

received, and at all of them there was a good attendance. These, I think, are the main achievements of the Club. They have been mainly concerned with internal growth.

In 1936 a new development took place which is, in my opinion, of considerable importance. The medical analysts[4] in London together with Gerhard Adler and Mr. (now Dr.) Wheelwright, who is at present in America, formed the Medical Society of Analytical Psychology; that society met to discuss clinical material and for other purposes which I shall mention later. Its existence provoked the lay analysts to meet on their own; this created tension, and the lay analysts eventually merged with the Medical Society, which changed its name to the Society of Practising Analysts.

The most outstanding achievement of the Medical Society was to formulate standards of training for analysts which received the approval of analysts in Zurich and which were publicly proclaimed as our standards at a meeting of the Medical Section of the British Psychological Society in 1939 by Dr. Baynes. The meeting was on the subject of lay analysis.

This achievement was another step forward. That group had no power to enforce its decisions and there was apparently too little libido contained there for its members to comply with its ordinances. In spite of this the records make a basis upon which we can build in the future. The group[5], which has not met for some time, will, I hope, reform itself and continue with the aim of raising the standards of work, improving the relationship between its members, and taking up questions of professional importance.

It will, I hope, be agreed that it is urgent for us to take up professional problems seriously because of the findings of our Committee which has been investigating the question of the Centre; it seems to me so important that I will anticipate the Committee's report and state its findings. There are now fifty 'analysts' in Britain who use the methods of analytical psychology. Some use more of it, some less. Amongst them are twenty lay 'analysts', which makes the position of medical men difficult, and

[4] Comprising Culver Barker, H. G. Baynes, Michael Fordham, James Kirsch, Violet de Laszlo, Erna Rosenbaum.

[5] By this time Dr. H. G. Baynes had died; Violet de Laszlo and J. Wheelwright were in the U.S.A.

so it has become increasingly important to have a group exerting some control over professional standards.

As a doctor I am often attacked for being an analytical psychologist, and I am anxious to be able to answer such statements as that Jungians are so irresponsible in professional matters that they are not worth consideration. I could answer such criticisms to my own satisfaction if I said that professional matters were in the hands of recognized analysts. Many of my medical colleagues, it is true, would look very askance at this, because they would think the practice of analysis ought to be a purely medical concern, but our movement has grown up with lay analysts, and this fact expresses its nature—it is not possible to deny that without damage to ourselves.

My idea is that the Analytical Psychology Club and the group of analysts could together form an embracing unity in which the varying aspects of analytical psychology could find expression; that they can be complementary to each other does not need amplification, except to say that there must always be a fundamental difference between those who are in daily contact with patients and those whose professional work is in another sphere.

So far the development of analytical psychology has been largely a spontaneous growth unhampered by many rules and regulations and not involving much group responsibility. It has, however, been based on a cohering central theme, the theme of the collective unconscious as a vital force in human life. The spontaneous way of development could, however, become destructive if it resisted the demands to organize more firmly which I believe are clearly indicated; we should ensure that this does not happen. Spontaneous vitality is a priceless gift which must be carried forward into any further stage of our development. That development consists, in my opinion and that of the Investigating Committee, in bringing the organic growth within the framework of an organization. In order to do this we must not allow the natural vitality to destroy the organizing purpose, but on the other hand we must not allow the organization to destroy the natural germinating vitality which springs from spontaneous impulse and reflection.

Let us now consider the various reasons for forming a centre in more detail.

First of all this is a period of organization where individualism stands less and less chance of survival, but where individuality in our sense needs to be expressed in a clear way. We should be denying the spirit of the times if we remained outside the collective developments, and I shall now consider some of the features of the recent moves in relation to medicine, because that profession has been stating its position and the Government has produced its White Paper on a Health Service. In considering pronouncements by the British Medical Association together with a recent statement by the Minister of Health I shall hope to show that starting a centre for ourselves would make a contribution towards current trends.

The British Medical Association has drawn up principles of medical practice which were approved by the Representative Meeting in September 1943. The first principle runs as follows:

The health of the people depends primarily upon the social and environmental conditions under which they work, upon security against fear and want, upon nutritional standards, upon educational facilities, and upon the facilities for exercise and leisure.

This expresses concisely the predominant attitude of the profession towards psychological and spiritual life: such features of our existence are not mentioned. Of course those who framed the proposals are not unaware of these factors but they are not thought of as the concern of medicine. They could be brought in under the next principle, which deals with treatment in general terms, but until the ideas for which we stand are built into the consciousness of official bodies there is ample scope for us to maintain our existence as a separate entity. The *British Medical Journal* scarcely ever prints papers on analytical topics, but a fair proportion of letters that appear therein are written by psychotherapists. The journal has always printed letters which I have submitted, and I have twice written in its pages on analytical psychology: once to deny a statement that we were becoming more and more of a religion. I was able to do this only as an individual, and it would carry much more weight if political questions could be dealt with by a representative body of analysts.

Analytical psychology is not of much significance to the medical profession. In a recent review of a book of mine[6] in the *British Medical Journal* I was referred to as 'one of the small

[6] *The Life of Childhood*, London, 1944.

group of medical psychologists practising in the country who *still*[7] follow the theories of Jung'. It is that 'still' which is so interesting, because it would seem to be part of a general effort to show that analytical psychology is an abortive attack on Freud which is gradually dying out. Individuals can never answer this kind of clever attack, but a corporate body denies it by its very existence.

I have mentioned these points to show our collective situation. It is a situation which needs a response from us. I do not believe the official attitude is unsympathetic.

The references to mental health in the government's White Paper are almost entirely to Mental Hospitals, the Lunacy Acts, and Mental Deficiency; analytical clinics are not mentioned at all. If we combine this fact with a speech made by the Right Hon. Ernest Brown, who was Minister of Health at the time, we shall see why this is so.

Mr. Brown's speech was made on 29 October 1943, at a Conference held by the Provisional National Council for Mental Health. He dealt with the amalgamation of various previously separate bodies interested in Mental Health movements; 'It is the Government's duty', he remarks, 'to give a lead, but, as I well know, legislation which is not backed by substantial public support tends to become unworkable and unworked.' That, then, is why our kind of work is left out; it is its unpopularity which makes it difficult for the Government to organize the Mental Health Services. Mr. Brown made it quite clear that it was the task of voluntary bodies to educate public opinion. 'Not the least important of the tasks which lie before the National Council', he says, 'is . . . the education of public opinion.' The National Council is now well established; it started from the amalgamation of small insignificant bodies.

If we were to start a centre we should be able to contribute more effectively to this educational aim; moreover, the fact of being able to refer patients to a clinic would be the most effective means of drawing the attention of the medical profession to the value of our work.

If I read the collective situation correctly, it is important for us not to delay too long if we wish to have a say in what is going on in this country. I should judge that we are, if not the only

[7] My italics.

unorganized group, at least one of the very few with anything to say at the present time, and if we remain unorganized I doubt whether we shall have any voice at all on the subject of Mental Health. Our introverted habit does not take very kindly to extraverted tactics, I mean to politics, but it is not necessary to push ourselves. I would like to put it in this way; let us give people more opportunity of knowing about analytical psychology, and let us not disdain the usual methods of doing so.

My second reason for starting a centre is the value a clinic would have in relation to the community. There are two clinics for the whole of London where thorough psychotherapeutic treatment is carried on: the Tavistock Clinic and the Institute of Psycho-Analysis. Both of them are getting many more patients than they can deal with; their waiting lists are long, and sometimes completely closed. If we take the out-patient departments of our major London hospitals, where a certain amount of psychotherapy is undertaken, we are confronted with a perfect deluge of patients whom we cannot see for more than a few minutes. Some of these patients are not suitable for analysis, but many of them are; there is nowhere to send them. The Child Guidance Clinics also provide a good chance of help for adult patients, for in these clinics the psychiatric social workers will offer assistance and some of them have themselves been analysed.

I have come to give up any expectation of treating the majority of patients who come needing help to the Child Guidance Clinics in which I have worked, and except in the most urgent cases I have had to adopt the policy of refusing to let the patient entertain any hope of treatment. I do this because I know that once the doors to the unconscious are opened and we do not undertake to go through the experiences which emerge, the patient will be in a worse position after our efforts than before. Most of my experience in clinics comes from the realm of child psychology, but the situation with regard to numbers of patients is far worse in the case of adults, as my knowledge of the Tavistock Clinic and St. Bartholomew's Hospital has shown me. It is true that there are a certain number of hospitals such as Woodside, the Cassel Hospital, and a number of private nursing homes that undertake in-patient treatment, but these are institutions for people with sufficient means.

If anyone doubts that these facts reveal the true state of affairs, he can look at the Faversham Report, which investigated the state of mental health services. It lists the defects in the existing clinics under the following six headings:

1. Defective staff arrangements.
2. Overcrowding and lack of time.
3. Lack of suitable accommodation.
4. Insufficient number of meetings (between doctors and patients).
5. Unsuitable locality.
6. Unsuitable selection of cases.

It is the most clear-cut statement about the situation in 1939 and there has been no significant change since then.

Quite apart therefore from producing the kind of treatment which our analysts would provide, there is a general need for patients to be treated; we could not attempt to fill the gap, but our contribution would help towards closing it.

Let us now turn to the internal benefits which may be expected to result from forming a centre. In the first place the Analytical Psychology Club would acquire a room of its own where it could hold its general meetings, its study groups, and its social gatherings. In the second place the room would be able to house the library, to which members would be able to gain access at any time of the day. This gain is considerable but it would also facilitate other developments, one of which I will suggest. I once discussed with a Spanish scholar, who was interested in Jung's ideas, what he thought he could get from a centre. He happened to be studying a Spanish author whose work was highly symbolical; he knew the Spanish setting, but he wanted to know the wider significance of certain of the symbols. If there was a place to which he could write and find out where to get the information he required, it would be of the greatest value to him, while I believe that his material could not fail to be of interest to us. I am sure that members could think of other advantages but I will not enumerate them here, because I want to deal mainly with our weaknesses and not our strength.

The gain to analysts and to the whole practice of analytical psychology would be an important one for the following reasons:

1. It would greatly help the training of analysts and make it possible to assess their practical capability by asking them to take patients under supervision. The details of such a scheme would

have to be worked out by the Medical group, but I have enough experience of training analysed and unanalysed persons in superficial and deep psychotherapeutic methods to know the value of a building, a definite meeting place, with time set apart for meetings, lectures and discussion groups.

Quite apart from the help which we as a body would get in ensuring that our analysts start off in their professional activities well equipped, the value to an analyst who wished to start would be very great. At present there is nowhere where the young analyst can get help in developing and improving his analytical technique, no clinic where he can even undertake analytical work in a satisfactory way; there is only his own private practice. It is not sufficiently realized, I think, that the actual analysis of patients is part of the making of an analyst. The personal training analysis, however thorough and satisfactory, can never be more than an indispensable prerequisite for becoming an analyst. The making of an analyst begins only when the candidate actually comes in touch with patients, and the growing pains which belong to this period need the aid of experienced analysts. It is on this point that I find it impossible to answer the criticism which I mentioned before, namely that we are irresponsible over the competence of our analysts, for it is substantially true. On the other hand it is not true that the actual standard of work done by our analysts is on the whole low; indeed the difficulties which stand in the way of practising have acted as a check on enthusiastic would-be analysts, and we have no reason as a body to feel inferior. There are, however, quite a number of what one might call para-Jungians about whose work we know little, and one reason for becoming a registered society is to make it more difficult for people to call themselves analytical psychologists and so to be identified with us. I may here comment that all sorts of practitioners have been known to call themselves by our name without any justification.

2. The next reason is our need to attract doctors who might become analysts. Our medical members are in a sense bound to do this, and in any case it is sound policy because of the essential unity between body and mind which needs to be held firmly in our consciousness and kept there. On the whole the medical profession, as we have seen, is predisposed to the materialistic and mechanistic interpretation of human nature, a view which

has been in evidence since the application of scientific method has won such gratifying victories over many diseases. Yet on account of this we have tended to disregard the substantial body of medical knowledge which may well help us in the approach to mental disorder. I have not myself much opinion of physical methods in the treatment of mentally deranged patients, but it is not at all impossible that one day good ones will become available. Psychological criteria are, and will remain, essential in their assessment.

Unfortunately the physical treatment of neurotic patients by the medical profession is at present too much in evidence, but it is not likely to continue with the same enthusiasm, and in the meantime it is desirable to keep voicing the view that the criteria for improvement or cure shall not be allowed to rest on objective or social grounds alone; the inner life of the patient must be taken seriously into account. Only medically trained analysts can support these contentions with any hope of respect from colleagues.

The criticism is familiar that lay analysts are liable to treat organic disease as though it were a mental phenomenon. Mistakes occur, but they occur in any case. I do not think lay analysts make them more often than do physicians or surgeons, and they can protect themselves by working in conjunction with doctors.

This brings us to review the collective trends we have to deal with in our support of lay analysis. When considering this matter I have in mind the idea of attracting doctors to our midst; fortunately the British Medical Association report deals precisely with lay analysis. The Committee on Psychotherapy by a majority vote was in favour of lay persons practising provided they worked under the supervision of a doctor. Unfortunately the recommendation was turned down by the Representative Committee and in the conclusion of their report published in 1941 it is stated that the Committee 'should regard it as its duty to promote with all its influence the training of adequate numbers of medical psychotherapists'. The Faversham Report, published in 1939, simply assumes that a medical training is necessary: 'For psychiatrists and psychotherapists the essential basis of all training is a registrable medical qualification.'[8] There has since appeared, in June 1943, a report of the Langdon-Brown Committee on Post-Graduate Training in Psychological Medicine. I

8 P. 204.

must say this makes odd reading, for it does not mention analysis of any kind from A to Z, though Dr. Edward Glover appears to have been on the Committee.

Other bodies which have some collective influence that expressed themselves on psychotherapy were the Anglican community and the English Free Churches, which were in favour of their members being trained, and were willing to co-operate with the medical profession; on the other hand the Roman Catholic community and the Church of Scotland were emphatically opposed to their members practising psychotherapy at all.

Thus we stand in a difficult position in relation to the collective bodies in Britain, but the situation which I have painted is not so dark as it seems. So far as I know, the Institute of Psycho-Analysis and ourselves are the only two groups which train lay analysts, but there is an increasing number of psychologists who are undertaking play therapy, which is a modified form of analysis; the psychologists are a fairly strong body, and it will be impossible to prevent a growing number of them giving treatment in Child Guidance Clinics all over the country. I think, however, that there is the fact that the case against lay analysts has never been very cogently stated; if this is, as I believe, because lay analysts do good work and have made considerable intellectual contributions to the body of knowledge, this will probably, in the end, get recognition.

To return to the question of attracting doctors: there are, it seems, a number of psychiatrists in the Forces who have gone far enough in our direction to be attracted by analysis, and if we are established when they come back many of them might well consider joining our circle. But it will not attract them, I think, unless our professional status is improved.

At this juncture it is necessary to meet the objection that some doctors will be put off by the existence of lay analysts amongst our number, and on the staff of any clinic we may start. I am sure that this is the case, but we have to consider whether we want doctors whose attitude is so prejudiced. Do we want members who are identified with their profession? We certainly should not look kindly on an analyst who was identified with analysis!

There is only one further reason for starting a centre which I want to consider, and that is the fact that a substantial amount of money has been promised. It will cover the initial expenses and half the income necessary to carry on for seven years. This is most encouraging if we are prepared to stand by the way of our development. It provides the means through which we could go further, because there is a reasonable expectation that we could raise more money if we really set out to do so. The promises of financial aid so far made have resulted from individual initiative only. Money ensures realistic thinking and makes action possible; it brings us down to earth; that is its main importance. The promises of financial aid demand down-to-earth response, and will of course be conditional on our becoming suitably organized. The danger of the money being available so early is that it might result in precipitate action. Action is required when our aims are clear and there is enough determination. What has been collected represents a reality to which we must respond or else lose, for no one will endure to have his spontaneous offers sniffed at or indefinitely postponed.

If we are going to use the money to the best advantage we shall need to become incorporated. This means that we become a registered Society and obtain the benefits which accrue from this course. These benefits are:

(1) It would give us a formal position and so improve our relationship with other bodies.
(2) It would limit the financial liability of members in the event of a failure to meet our commitments.
(3) It would facilitate the collection of further financial aid.

Incorporation is a serious matter, and requires much thought about the structure of the Society, how it is going to be run, and what its aims are going to be. The aims particularly require careful consideration, because they have to be set out in a special document, the Memorandum of Association, which can only be altered by Act of Parliament.

More detailed consideration of these matters can wait, but I mention them now because there will be plenty of opportunity for those careful or fearful souls who love the details of procedure to ensure a thoroughly sound basis for the Society.

This brings me to the next part of my paper, in which I want to give my own idea of the structure of a society which would meet the requirements of the external world and at the same

O   193

time continue the development which has been proceeding in the past.

The Analytical Psychology Club has its basis, its history, and its methods: it could form one part of the centre without any change. On the other hand the analysts must have complete control of the clinic, and thus must be separate from the Club. That will involve creating another body which would ultimately be responsible for the policy of the centre as a whole. The composition of this body, which might be called a council, is clearly a controversial matter, but I would like to put forward the idea that both for internal and external reasons it should have a controlling majority of practising analysts in order to ensure our professional status.

Before concluding I would like briefly to discuss another idea which I think was first put forward at the previous club meeting. The idea was this: Would it not be better to leave the club out of it and start a clinic alone? I fear that if this were done it would undermine the whole statement of what we mean. If analytical psychology could be considered simply as a branch of medicine, a kind of medical speciality, then it would be feasible; but this is not at all the nature of our development. It would, or so it seems to me, deal a blow at an important meaning of the Club, whose aims are set forth as follows: 'It shall establish contact between persons interested in analytical psychology and shall carry out the study of and research into analytical psychology and associated fields.'

Let me enumerate some of these 'associated fields': besides the medical one, which has already been sufficiently dealt with, there are the fields of religion, education, anthropology, art, and literature.

Analytical psychology is a fundamental form of experience and knowledge, a science of human nature taking as its basic postulate the psyche;[9] it has its own field and its own method, and so cannot be understood as a specialized branch of something else. We are not just specialists, for specialism is a way of confining the living process. If we do this, we are lost for ever to wider considerations and to essential human issues. Specialism is liable to become the graveyard which contains the corpses of

[9] Cf. Jung, 'Basic Postulates of Analytical Psychology', *Modern Man in Search of a Soul*. London, 1933.

promising youth; we may contemplate that graveyard so long as it brings us to realize our own life. Let us therefore consider the idea of forming a separate clinic only to reject it firmly, holding fast to the conception of analytical psychology as a living whole with a centre which expresses its individuality.

INDEX

P   209